British Prehistory

STUART PIGGOTT

Professor of Prehistoric Archæology in the University
of Edinburgh

Geoffrey Cumberlege

OXFORD UNIVERSITY PRESS

LONDON   NEW YORK   TORONTO

First published 1949 *and reprinted in* 1955

PRINTED IN GREAT BRITAIN

INTRODUCTORY NOTE

ANY attempt at a work of synthesis of this kind must be to a large extent a compilation from the work of others, and to all those who have recorded primary material, or made interpretations of it over a part or the whole of the field covered by this book, my debt is obvious. In so short a treatment of a subject which contains so many unresolved problems I have had to adopt a more dogmatic phraseology than I should have liked, but it is impossible to qualify the reconstruction of events at almost every turn with some indication that they represent at best an approximation to a probability. The reader should therefore keep at the back of his mind the proviso that any interpretation of the sequence of British (and indeed of European) prehistory must be thought of as representing the most likely explanation of a set of facts and observed phenomena *in the present state of our knowledge.* The serious study of prehistory is scarcely half a century old, and it is only by putting forward working hypotheses that we can hope to reconstruct the life of the primitive communities whose handiwork in pottery or metal, in stone or earthwork, remains to-day as their only tangible heritage.

December 1948.   S. P.

5

NOTE TO SECOND IMPRESSION

THE dissatisfaction with the Piltdown finds, felt for some years by most anatomists and archæologists and expressed on p. 38, has now been confirmed by the scientific investigations which show it to have been an elaborate fake: the results are set out in J. S. Weiner's *The Piltdown Forgery* (Oxford University Press, 1955).

S. P.

1955

CONTENTS

CHAPTER I

ARCHÆOLOGICAL TECHNIQUE AND THE NATURE OF THE EVIDENCE

THE study of the prehistoric past is one of sufficiently recent growth for its techniques, the nature of the evidence it employs, and the information it builds up to be unfamiliar. For this reason some sort of a preface to a book on prehistoric Britain is essential if the reader who is not an archæologist is to grasp the limitations, no less than the potential scope, of the methods employed, and to understand something of the prehistorian's approach. The methods of the historian working on the written record have been appreciated by most educated persons since history began to be compiled, and such an introduction would be unnecessary in an historical survey; but while the prehistorian and historian work along parallel lines, and the former can extend the perspective of human culture several millennia beyond the reach of the written record, the nature of the material he employs leads him to view man's story from a standpoint from which is excluded, save by inference, the knowledge of human thought and motive which the historian finds contained in his contemporary sources.

The history of archæological research in Britain is interesting and significant, and serves to explain the nature of some of the sources we now use. Apart from sporadic medieval antiquarianism, attention to prehistoric antiquities was first directed by the great figures of English local historical studies, such as Camden and

Dugdale, who recorded a conspicuous earthwork or megalithic monument between descriptions of a castle and an abbey, usually with a vague attribution to the Danes or the Romans. That engaging and whimsical dilettante of the late seventeenth century, John Aubrey, was an indefatigable collector of the odd and curious— a ghost story, a fantastic anecdote, a piece of folk-lore —but when he turned to prehistoric antiquities his collecting of notes came as near to system and method as his grasshopper mind could ever achieve, and his observations on such Wessex monuments as Stonehenge and Avebury are still of value, and show the beginning of what has become a great British tradition in archæology, the study of field monuments by observation and survey without excavation. This tradition was carried on in the early eighteenth century by William Stukeley, who brought a vivid appreciation of English topography and terrain to bear on his more detailed surveys of monuments and areas already sketched out by Aubrey, but who vitiated much of his early achievement by wild theorizing on the basis of his earlier field-work.

But by the beginning of the nineteenth century a new trend was perceptible. Field archæology fitted naturally enough into the Romantic revival—the tour in search of the picturesque was incomplete without a Druids' altar, and ancient barrows and cairns were, after Ossian, coming into their own as fit objects of melancholy contemplation—and with this new interest in the wild barbarian past came the urge to find out more by digging up some authentic Ancient British relics. The occasional excavation of a barrow became a feature of English country-house life, and some squires devoted much of their energies to this new hobby—Sir Richard Colt

Hoare and his henchman, Mr. Cunnington, dug indefatigably in Wiltshire from 1794 to 1810; Mr. Thomas Bateman of Youlgreave in Derbyshire spent ten years from 1848 in the same pursuit. They collected the less perishable finds from their diggings into private museums, they published some account of their discoveries, and they were esteemed redoubtable antiquaries in their day. By the middle of the century the county archæological societies were being formed, often partly tractarian and ecclesiological, and not a few country parsons entered the ranks of the antiquaries and diggers—Canon Greenwell of Durham dug extensively in Yorkshire and elsewhere, forming an enormous collection later acquired by the British Museum, and published an account of his activities in 1877; while it is typical of the changing social structure of Victorian England that his successor in Yorkshire barrow-digging, from about 1860 to the end of the century, was a self-made corn merchant of Driffield, J. R. Mortimer.

Side by side with the diggers, the collectors. It was upon them, rather than upon the excavators of barrows, that Victorian geology impinged, and with it the concepts of stratigraphy and the evolution of types. Both the geologist and the archæological collector benefited from, and were in some sense the outcome of, the great constructional works of canal digging and railway embankment and cutting activity, which exposed the earth's strata in section and produced a rich haul of fossils and antiquities. The concept of an ordered succession in prehistoric antiquities based on a stone-bronze-iron sequence seems to have been originated by Thomsen, a Danish museum-curator in the eighteen-thirties, but the evolutionary background implied was to receive fresh impetus from Darwin's classic statement of 1859. This was taken up by antiquaries such as Lubbock in the eighteen-sixties, and was given decisive canonization by the great collector-typologist, Sir John Evans, in his two books on stone and bronze implements in 1872 and 1881.

The result of this century of activity was that by the eighteen-nineties there was a relatively vast accumulation of prehistoric antiquities in private collections or local museums, vaguely regarded as belonging to three periods, the Stone Age (the earlier part of which the orthodox styled Pre-Diluvian, the more daring recognized as of geological antiquity), the Bronze Age, and the Iron Age. These technological stages in the history of human tools and weapons were regarded as the result of an ordered evolution within Britain, and about the one certain date was that of Julius Cæsar's invasion, which was agreed to have terminated the Iron Age by introducing an era of written history to these islands. These nineteenth-century collections still remain and, it must be remembered, still form the raw material for much of our prehistory. The excavations which produced the antiquities are by modern standards hopelessly inadequate: the circumstances of finding are frequently recorded so vaguely as to be useless as evidence. Very little attention was paid to the structures in which the burials were found, when these antiquities are the result of barrow-digging, and only the more durable survived the navvy's pickaxe. But they do give a great corpus of material from all over Britain which could never be recovered to-day in such bulk, when more exacting technique would only permit of a tiny proportion of the sites being excavated with the time and funds available—they give certain important generalities on which we can still work.

By the end of the last century, then, progress in British archæology was obstructed by two barriers—the lack of excavation technique which would extract the maximum information from the site under investigation, and the need of historical synthesis of the available material from a European standpoint, which would test the theory of an insular evolutionary sequence. Lieutenant-General Pitt-Rivers, retiring in the eighteen-eighties to his Wessex estates, brought a mind of unconventional vigour to deal objectively with the first problem, and, with capital and experience of organization at his command, built up the technique of scientific excavation in a manner which still calls for bewildered admiration. ' Up rise ye then, our barrow-digging men, For 'tis our opening day ', sang the poetaster commemorating Bateman's excavations in Derbyshire already referred to, but in no such light-hearted picnic spirit were the General's excavations conducted, when the site was surveyed with tape and level, and elaborately contoured by his staff of technicians, who were again ready, when the trained workmen had commenced the actual digging, to record the finding of every potsherd or piece of bone. And then, when the entire site had been stripped and excavated to the unbroken soil at every point, they were to compile the great detailed reports, with their plans and sections, their statistical tables and their analytical indices. Modern excavation technique is essentially based on the work of Pitt-Rivers, which established the principle that an excavation is a scientific experiment which can never be repeated on the particular site involved, so that every possible scrap of detail must be wrung out of the soil, and presented objectively in a published report.

The new approach to the interpretation of archæological material was established at about the same time
by a Scot, the Hon. John Abercromby, who turned his
attention to the British Bronze Age, largely represented
by the very large collection of pottery amassed during the
nineteenth century by the barrow-digging squires and
clergy whose activities we have already noticed. Abercromby made a systematic collection of the relevant
material in a corpus of illustrations and details, beginning on a distinctive type of vessel which he proposed
calling a Beaker, and which he perceived, from a study
of the continental evidence, to have very close affinities
across the English Channel. In a classic paper, first read
to the British Association at Belfast in 1902, he postulated
the arrival in south and east England of invaders from
the Continent at the beginning of the Bronze Age (early
in the second millennium B.C.), bringing with them the
tradition of making these characteristic pottery vessels
from their homeland on the Rhine or in the Low
Countries. This implied a revolution in the concept of
prehistory, with the interplay of migration and trade
across the European continent as an important factor
in the evolution of cultures: the processes known from
the historical record to have formed the pattern of
European civilization at a later date could now be
perceived at work in the remote past, and the geographical aspect of the distribution of cultures in space as
well as in time began to receive attention. The likelihood
of other prehistoric immigrations into Britain became
recognized, and by the nineteen - twenties Britain was
seen as a part of the general stream of European
prehistory.

What then is our position to-day? Our source-material

must still remain in part the objects recovered by un-scientific digging in the past: analytical and comparative study based on large series of tools or pots must utilize this material to a great extent. Our knowledge of such things as house-plans, or details of funerary ritual, must, however, depend on accurate and painstaking excavation in the Pitt-Rivers tradition—here in fact the greatest gaps in our knowledge occur, as they also tend to occur in regions where excavation, or even antiquarian digging, has been little carried out. The material from the old collections will often yield important additional information by the application of new scientific techniques—a thin section of a stone axe under the geological microscope may reveal the source of its manufacture in a region remote from its finding-place, and so give information on trade; so too may chemical analysis of the metal ores in a bronze dagger. Detailed examination of the surface of a pot by a trained botanist may reveal the casts of cereal grains accidentally incorporated at the time of making and burnt out in firing, and so throw valuable light on early agriculture.

We may compare the processes of prehistoric and historic research in this respect. If one uses prehistory as a convenient term for the interpretation and synthesis of the material relics of ancient man, one may term the techniques which obtain the prehistorian's source-material, archæology; and though prehistory and archæology are to this extent distinct, they are mutually interdependent, and the scientific disciplines utilized by the archæologist to obtain his evidence are as essential as palæography and the use of ultra-violet photographs are to an historian studying a palimpsest. The original documents of the historian are represented in the prehistorian's work by an excavated site, or objects in a museum, but while some of his work will be based on original research of this kind, he must also depend on the equivalent of the historian's calendars of documents and published texts, in his case excavation reports or the published illustrations of museum specimens. The historian again can use his knowledge of contemporary legal procedure or administrative functions to interpret the past from its documents, and the prehistorian can often come nearer to an understanding of the works of ancient man by comparison with modern primitives (within which may be included Australian blackfellows and Hebridean crofters!). Archæology is to prehistory what palæography and the study of diplomatic are to history, but overwhelmingly more important, since the interpretation of archæological evidence is so much more technical and involved than that of historical documents.

It must be admitted that the picture which can be reconstructed from archæological evidence is inevitably one-sided and limited. The material of archæology depends on the accident of survival, and so varies in its content from place to place. Normally perishable materials such as textiles or wood may be preserved by unusual dryness and desiccation in Sinkiang or Arizona, by moisture in Denmark or the Caucasus, by freezing in Greenland or the Altai—in Britain moisture is the only exceptional preservative factor, and normally only the relatively imperishable substances such as stone, metal, and sometimes bone survive.

This applies equally to portable objects of human manufacture—tools and weapons, pots, jewellery and ornaments—which in the past received the greater attention, and to structures such as houses, fortifications, or tombs. Here the perishable materials may leave at least a negative record in the soil—a timber-built house will either be made on a framework of upright posts set firmly into sockets dug into the ground, or less commonly on a beam framework sunk in sleeper-trenches, and although the wood may rot to powder, the softer discoloured filling of post-hole or sleeper-trench will remain to be identified by the archæologist. The development of technique in excavation has been directed to the detection and elucidation of just such traces of perished materials, and does permit at least of the recovery of ground-plans of otherwise vanished structures, and by estimation of the size of the timbers, implied by the diameter of the post-holes, some indication of the appearance above ground can be gained. By painstaking excavation the most surprisingly evanescent happenings can be recovered after the lapse of millennia. Careful cleaning of an excavated floor in Mesopotamia revealed the hoof-prints of the sacrificial sheep and the foot-prints of the men who had dug their heels into the soft clay floor as they held the animals in ancient Sumerian times, about 2500 B.C.; under the covering mound of Bronze Age barrows in Denmark and Holland of about 1500 B.C. were found the marks made by cross-ploughing at right angles with a primitive plough—the burials had been made in cultivated fields. Sometimes a curious chance will give us unexpected information as when, in the Late Neolithic in Orkney, the inhabitants built in the easily split local stone the dressers and bedsteads it would be normal elsewhere to make in wood, and so provided us with a permanent indication of their form.

Prehistory therefore uses the techniques of archæology,

especially excavation, to obtain its raw material, and it is in fact wholly dependent on such archæological evidence. The modern developments in archæological research have been mainly directed towards the application of scientific disciplines in the elucidation of its material, and a close collaboration is now being built up between the archæologist and workers in the natural sciences. An excavator may profitably use an electrical resistivity survey of the area he is to dig in order to find out the disposition of disturbed soil and filled-up ditches before he plans his actual cuttings into the soil. Indications of such ancient features can also be obtained in many instances by air observation and photography of the site covered with a growing crop, which responds to disturbed soil by a stronger and darker growth. Collaboration with geologists and botanists may make it possible to establish the human occupation of a site in its relationship with the natural land-movements or (geologically speaking) recent deposits—considerable work on these lines has been carried out in the East Anglian fenland, where human occupation from the Mesolithic period through successive stages of culture up to the Roman Occupation in the first centuries A.D. has been studied in its relationship to the land movements and the formation of peat over this long period of time. The study of the earlier phases of prehistory (the Palæolithic period, going backwards in time for immense epochs from about 15,000 B.C.) is inextricably bound up with geology and the deposition of natural deposits such as gravels laid down by rivers formed by the melting ice during the periodic withdrawal of the great ice-sheets.

The application of the techniques of soil study have provided illuminating information on ancient soil-surfaces which may for instance be sealed under a prehistoric burial mound or the rampart of a fortification —it may be possible to tell whether the soil was formed under dry or wet climatic conditions, or whether it had been tilled for agricultural purposes. Here, too, analysis of the phosphate content may afford a clue to vanished organic matter implying manure or the debris of primitive occupation. The botanical study of the pollen contained in peat deposits has enabled the sequence of forest history in northern Europe from the final withdrawal of the ice-sheet about 8000 B.C. to be determined in great detail in relationship to human occupation. Not only can the constituents of the forests growing in the neighbourhood of the pools in which peat was forming, and into which the tree pollen was wind-blown, be detected, but also the pollen of weeds associated with cultivation, and the presence of ancient arable land in the neighbourhood inferred.

An interesting example of the use of scientific techniques was recently shown by a study of a find of ' bog-butter ' in Scotland—a wooden keg filled with a fatty material found in a peat-bog. Such finds have frequently been made in the past, and are traditionally said to be butter, and are mainly of medieval or later date; but in this instance, and in other samples examined by chemists specializing in fat analysis, no chemical constituents characteristic of butter could be found. It was pointed out that these could have vanished through natural causes, and attention was next paid to the impurities in the substance, which were mostly hairs (one begins to understand the words of the medieval drinking song, ' Bring us in no butter, for it is full of hairs '). Under the microscope of the zoologist these hairs proved to be mainly those of red cattle, of typical Highland kyloe type, a few of dogs, and some long human hairs which implied the presence of blonde and auburn dairymaids. Such a collection of hairs was so natural to a none-too-scrupulous dairy of the Dark Ages or medieval times, that the traditional attribution of these kegs of fat to butter received considerable confirmation, which the chemists had been unable to supply owing to the evaporation of certain essential constituents in the course of time.

A combination of archæological research and that of the petrologist examining rocks in south-west England has been establishing important facts about the trade in axes made of the hard tough stones of west Britain into such areas as the Wessex chalk, where such stone does not occur. Archæologically it was established that such axes were being used in Wessex about 2000–1800 B.C., and the geologists on their side showed that the stones from which such tools were made (basing their observations on a representative series of over 350 specimens) came in the main from three localities, in Cornwall, North Wales, and the Lake District respectively—in those places only were the exact types of rocks found naturally. A most valuable contribution to our knowledge of early trade was therefore made: some years ago a similar piece of work showed the source of the 'Blue Stones' at Stonehenge to be the Presely Range in Pembrokeshire.

Somewhat similar methods can be used for metals and other substances when analysed by means of burning a very small portion in an arc and photographing the resulting spectrum. In this way minute proportions of elements present as impurities can be detected, and by comparing spectra, these proportions can be matched in two or more instances, thus implying a common origin for substances having identical impurities in identical proportions. By this means metal ores may be traced to their source, and a particularly important result obtained by spectrographic analysis was to prove the identity of composition of beads of faience (a complicated artificial substance incorporating a glass frit) from British Bronze Age graves and from Ancient Egypt. The Egyptian beads (identical in appearance also with the British and other European finds) can be dated by written records to about 1380 B.C., so that these beads imported from the Ancient East into barbarian Europe constitute a factor of great importance in working out our prehistoric chronology.

By such means as the foregoing, archæologists are constantly seeking to redress to some degree the inevitable incompleteness of the story told by the chance survival of certain objects of human material culture. These techniques can, of course, be applied to the investigation of any phase of human culture, whether in the past beyond the written record or in the less understood aspects of the historical period—as when the sequence of the styles and manufacture of Bristol ' Delft ' in the eighteenth century A.D. was elucidated by excavations of the old potters' kilns at Brislington.

By means such as those briefly noticed, the archæologist endeavours to build up as complete a picture as he can of the material culture of the people he is studying in his excavation or by his analytical treatment of groups of relics. In archæological terminology the word ' culture ' is employed as a convenient term for the aggregate of comparable factors which can be traced in the material equipment of more than one site—it may be indicated by a common type of settlement (farmsteads or villages of closely grouped houses), house-plans (circular huts or oblong cabins), agricultural systems (square fields cross-ploughed with a light plough, or in long strips by a heavy animal-drawn one), types of tombs (in cemeteries or singly, by cremation or by unburnt burial—inhumation), and above all in types of tools and pottery. Only large-scale excavation can reveal the lay-out of a complete village or even of one house; the survival of traces of an agricultural system is determined to a large extent by the degree modern farming has obliterated the ancient field-boundaries; and tomb-types again can only be recovered by excavation. But the common objects of everyday life in prehistoric times survive by their very commonness — flint implements can be picked up on ploughed fields after rain, and potsherds collected from mole-heaps and rabbit-scrapes without any process of excavation, archæological or commercial. Pitt-Rivers laid down the doctrine that ' what is important is what is persistent ', and broken pottery—useless, almost indestructible—is the most persistent object from which the archæologist can deduce his groups of peoples united by a common material culture.

In primitive societies pottery-making is a craft bound by rigid conservatism. An archæologist wishing to understand the technique of primitive ceramics apprenticed herself to the potter in a modern Egyptian village, whose repertoire of shapes was limited to certain stock forms decreed by tradition. Gaining command of her craft, she one day produced a pot of a shape both pleasing and useful, but outside the accepted series. On submitting this for approval to the potter she was met with the response, 'There is only one way you *may* make a pot' for such-and-such a purpose, and the offending innovation was smashed with decisive finality. It is this intense traditionalism that enables archæologists to use pottery as an index to cultural groups and their movements. The Early Bronze Age 'Beakers' studied by Abercromby are an excellent example of this—they are particularly formalized and consistent vessels, with texture and ornament which can be recognized in tiny fragments, and their association with other cultural traits having now been established, we make use of them to denote allied groups of people conveniently referred to as Beaker folk, under this term including not only the actual makers of these vessels, but an agricultural and pastoral people, burying their dead by inhumation in single graves, using copper and bronze axes and daggers, living in villages of circular houses and worshipping in open circular sanctuaries. All these factors together go to make up the Beaker culture, but the most common and persistent, from the archæologist's point of view, is the pottery style itself.

Pottery-making appears as an innovation in Europe, in the main derived from the Ancient East with other elements of village and farming life from about 3000 B.C. onwards; and for the enormous Old Stone Age periods preceding these advances in the craft of living, our persistent objects are tools of stone. Here the space-dimension is as tremendous as that of time, and we can only see the broadest distinctions in cultures, which on the evidence of the types of stone tools may stretch from the Thames to the Indus, and southwards to the Cape, or cover the whole Eurasiatic land-mass from Russia to China.

Within the cultural groups the archæologist endeavours to reconstruct so far as he is able the social structure of the societies with which he is dealing. If a prehistoric village is completely excavated and shows no marked disparity in the sizes of the huts nor any system of lay-out with relation to any one building, one may reasonably infer a community of peasants living on terms of approximate equality without the concentration of wealth and power into the hands of any one individual or chieftain. Cemeteries of graves which do not include burials more richly provided for the future life with tools or pots than the majority, would indicate the same social structure—the Late Bronze Age cemeteries in south England about 750 B.C. are good examples of this. Inferences of this kind can be drawn only when excavation has been complete and competent—the prehistoric cities in western India of c. 2500 B.C. were claimed as examples of primitive communism until new excavations in 1946 brought to light within the cities the defended citadels that implied forceful centralized rule.

Again, types of early social organization known to us from ancient literature may be recognizable — the 'heroic' warrior aristocracy known from Homer, from the Viking sagas, and from the early Celtic literature, can be found reflected in the Viking graves with their warlike furnishings, or the chariot burials of the Celtic Iron Age of the third century B.C. in Yorkshire; and when in Bronze Age Wessex about 1500 B.C. we find the graves of men richly equipped with great bronze daggers and gold and amber trappings, and even in a couple of instances with ceremonial maces or sceptres of authority, we may reasonably conclude that here again are the burials of a 'heroic' dynasty which established power over, and exploited the natural resources of, the region in which they ruled.

The necessary framework into which these pictures of primitive social groups must be fitted is that of chronology. The earlier antiquaries could only make vague guesses as to the antiquity of human culture beyond the record of written history in Europe, and as far as England was concerned this meant, with the exception of a few mentions in Greek travellers and geographers, little beyond Cæsar and Tacitus. It became clear at the end of the last century that the Old Stone Age cultures belonged to a very remote period of time, before the geography of the European continent had taken on its present form, but for the later periods there were no clues. We now have two main methods of establishing the chronology of barbarian Europe before the introduction of the written record: the first by correlation with the natural time-scale of the geologists and palæobotanists; the second by a series of links with the cultures of the Ancient East, where recorded history in terms of solar years can be established to about 3000 B.C.

The natural time-scale is our only framework for the Palæolithic and much of the ensuing Mesolithic periods, and some geologists, using the astronomical calculations of the variations in solar radiation over past millennia, have equated these with recurrent phases of heat and cold (the Ice Ages) and constructed a chronological scheme of dating in years before the present time to the first Ice Age, about six hundred thousand years ago. The final retreat of the ice-sheet in northern Europe from about 10,000 B.C. resulted in the annual deposition of melt-water mud which now in Scandinavia forms distinctive banded clays: the bands can be counted and one sequence equated with another until a series is built up carrying the series on until recent times. In that region too, and in Britain, the sequence of forest history after the amelioration of the climate permitted trees to grow on the former steppe land has been worked out by the system of pollen-analysis of peat deposits already referred to; and the changing woodland composition from a dominance of birch to one of pine, followed by the establishment of a mixed oak forest, has been fitted into the known sequence of human cultures between the Mesolithic (from 10,000 B.C.) through the Neolithic, Bronze, and Iron Ages, and the dawn of history.

This time-scale is, however, too coarse when dealing with cultures whose composition changed with immigration and trade contacts within a relatively few generations, and it also depends on the necessary archæological finds being made in circumstances in which they can be linked with natural deposits such as peat-beds. We have therefore to turn to the concept of the zoning of cultures in descending scales of technological achievement beyond the primary centres of early civilization. The elements of agricultural life, soon followed by the discovery of the techniques of metal-working, were established in the Ancient East by the fifth millennium B.C., and from this region there was a gradual spread across the European continent of the basic concepts of agricultural economy among the primitive communities of hunters and food-gatherers who formed the descendants of the Palæolithic men. These were faced with the necessity of modifying their habits of life now that the climatic conditions had changed, cutting down their hunting grounds and causing the disappearance of their quarry by extinction or migration to other regions.

We can trace this slow spread of agricultural village communities to Britain, either by the land-routes across the Continent, or by the coasting sea-ways of the west. The complicated craft of metal-working was more slow in its spread than that of the stock-breeder or cultivator or potter, so that the first farming communities in north Europe and Britain are in a Stone Age without the use of metal tools. It is possible to assign dates to the non-literate cultures of stone or early metal-using peoples around the Mediterranean or along the Middle Danube by their use of types of tools, ornaments, or pots related to those in the Near East from which they were in fact derived—this often of course only fixes the earliest possible date at which a given type could have come into use, and allowance has to be made for long survival of a style or technique, or even of an actual object. Jewellery may be handed down for generations before it is deposited with the last of the line in a grave, and a warrior's sword may likewise be passed from father to son (as we know for instance from the evidence of the sagas, confirmed by finds in Viking graves).

It is this realization that the prehistoric cultures of Britain are closely tied to those of the European main-land, and thence to the literate civilizations of the Eastern Mediterranean, that Abercromby first made possible by his study of British Bronze Age pottery. We may sometimes be fortunate, and find for instance in a grave of a European prehistoric barbarian some object obtained by trade, or in the well-known ancient custom of the interchange of presents between chieftains, which really comes from the ancient Orient, where it can be accurately dated. The blue faience beads already mentioned, known from many Bronze Age graves in Europe, and accurately paralleled only by certain Egyptian (and possibly Palestinian) beads of a known date about 1380 B.C., form therefore invaluable checks on the dating of the Bronze Age cultures in which they occur. Or the reverse may happen—the great shaft graves of Mycenæ contained among their treasures amber beads of a type and substance only found in northern Europe, and these must represent trade with the north. The date of these graves and others in which similar amber has been found is fixed at about 1600 B.C. by Egyptian and other contacts, and consequently the dating of the comparable examples in the north is set within reasonable limits.

By such means as this, and by a constant checking and comparison between the objects produced by the various prehistoric cultures, a chronological scale is being built up, always subject to revision but fairly well established in its broad outlines in Britain. Within these outlines, however, it is very often difficult to work out local correlations in detail: here the geographical factor may be of great importance in evaluating local sequences, for a culture imposed by invasion in southern Britain at some approximately determined date may take some centuries to spread and appear in the remote-north-west among the mountains—but here again one must be prepared for other cultural innovations finding their way much more swiftly by sea-routes, and coming in by the back door, so to speak.

Nor must we forget that similar evolutionary processes may take place independently in different areas, producing for instance types of social organization perceptible in the archæological record (such as the ' heroic ' cultures mentioned above) which are parallel to, but not derived one from another. The tendency to think in terms of these several similar evolutions of human society is of course clearly perceptible in the Russian interpretation of prehistory from the viewpoint of Marxist philosophy.

For the purposes of this book, however, we may bear in mind a rough chronological sequence for Britain as follows. The Palæolithic (Old Stone) Age was one of primitive hunting and food-gathering economy and may have begun some six hundred thousand years ago, when we see the first appearance of man-made stone tools in geological deposits. Vast climatic variations of heat and great cold took place until the ice-sheet settled within the Arctic Circle about 10,000 B.C. With the spread of forests the hunters modified their life, but still remained dependent on the chase—this is the Mesolithic stage, and lasted in Britain until about 2300 B.C. or a little earlier, when the first agriculturists began to arrive across the comparatively newly formed English Channel (formed by about 6000 B.C.) and on the west coasts. These were the bearers of Neolithic (New Stone Age) culture, and within a few centuries were receiving fresh drafts of immigrants who made use of the copper and tin deposits of West Britain and Ireland in an Early Bronze Age about 1900 B.C. The Bronze Age continued with minor incursions of peoples from the Continent until, first soon after 1000, and then in about 750 B.C., important Late Bronze Age immigrations took place which were in a sense heralds of the iron-using cultures which were established about 400 B.C. as the Early Iron Age, which, again with various immigrant movements, continued until the exploratory raids of Cæsar in the first century B.C. and the Roman Conquest of A.D. 43.

CHAPTER II

THE PALÆOLITHIC AND MESOLITHIC PERIODS

THERE is a quality of inhuman remoteness about the Palæolithic period that makes its position as the necessary introduction to any scheme of prehistory a rather painful one to the ordinary reader. The enormous time-scale, which constitutes an excursion into geological and astronomical systems of chronology, is one outside the reasonable human comprehension—to say that a type of extinct man was making stone implements five or six hundred thousand years ago can mean very little to most of us beyond a vague appreciation of an immense (but inconceivable) duration; while the slowness of human progress during those remote times, when implements of practically identical type continue to be made, as the outcome of a presumably equally unchanging social economy, for ten or twenty thousand years, involves concepts that can only be appreciated by a mind habituated to the vast eras of geology. Similes can be roughly suggested which perhaps imply the time-scale, on the lines that if the Siege of Troy took place yesterday, the beginning of the Palæolithic would have been more than six months ago, but beyond these approximations it is difficult to do more than to state the figures which have been given, on the basis of astronomical calculation of the solar radiation curve in the past, as a chronological framework for the Palæolithic, and leave the reader to find his own way of grasping their magnitude if he can.

The figures are after all an approximation, and their exact application to the recent geological sequence is not universally accepted, but what is important to grasp is that the earliest stages in human progress were of immense duration, and that technological advance as estimated by the changes in the styles and modes of manufacture of stone implements was proportionately slow. Furthermore, the geographical aspect must be borne in mind — the earliest human societies were relatively so undifferentiated that a uniform material culture may be observed stretching across whole continents and taking on a virtually identical appearance in England, Africa, or India. This uniformity illustrates one aspect of the Palæolithic cultures—the movements of small hunting groups over very large territories, and the lack of a sufficiently stable food-producing economy to permit communities settling in comparatively restricted areas and there evolving a locally distinctive form of culture.

The term Palæolithic is used to define a large group of humanly made tools and weapons, and in some instances structures such as houses or graves, which may or may not be directly associated with actual fossil human bones, but all of which occur in natural geological deposits belonging to the Pleistocene phase—an epoch having a duration which is estimated as beginning about six hundred thousand and ending perhaps ten or fifteen thousand years ago. The whole of the remainder of human prehistory and history is contained in the geological phase of the Holocene (or Recent) period, and this (in which we still live to-day) is, with the Pleistocene, grouped as the Quaternary period of the four great major divisions of the earth's history. The word Quaternary may then be regarded as indicating the broadest concept of man's place in the whole organic sequence on the planet; the Pleistocene gives further precision to the geological period with which we are concerned, and our immediate study is that of Palæolithic man and his manufactures ('industries' for groups of tools of comparable types and techniques; 'cultures' for aggregates of material elements surviving to show the social structure of a human group — dwelling-places, tools, ornaments, burials).

The long duration of the Pleistocene period can be subdivided in a natural time-scale based on the remarkable and violent climatic fluctuations that can be traced in the northern hemisphere, with their probable repercussions in the tropics. A variety of causes within the solar system, still imperfectly understood but certainly largely bound up with the variations in the sun's radiation, seem to have resulted in a cycle of fluctuations in temperature and climate between comparative heat and intense cold, though we do not know why this particular series of climatic variations should have begun in the Pleistocene: the astronomical theory explains the sequence of the fluctuations, but not their cause. But their implications were enormous and far-reaching, and though the changes were so spread over the centuries that they would have been imperceptible to any one generation of men, their effect on the course of human prehistory was very great. At least four times during the time when man can be distinguished as a distinct species, the ice-sheet, now the Polar cap within the Arctic Circle, spread southwards until it covered much of northern Europe, effectually preventing any human or animal colonization of large tracts of land and rendering the climate arctic or sub-arctic in a broad belt along its southern fringe. At its maximum the ice covered all Ireland and came southward in England to a line roughly through Gloucester, Warwick, north of London, through Ipswich and thence approximately to Cologne, Cracow, and Kiev; at its minimum it exposed a small part of southern Ireland, some of West Wales, and England south of an irregular line stretching up to Yorkshire. In Europe the ice capped the Alps to a lower snow-line than to-day, and the main sheet had its edge on a line through Hamburg, Berlin, north of Warsaw, and south of Vilna, and covering the area now the Baltic Sea.

These great glaciations, or Ice Ages, with the warmer intervals, or Interglacial periods, form a giant chronological scale against which the Palæolithic humans and their remains can be set. The glacial and interglacial stages of the Pleistocene are by no means of equal duration—the Second Interglacial was nearly four times as long as the others, and is sometimes known as the Great Interglacial for that reason—and the glaciations are themselves complex, the first, second, and third having each two well-marked maxima, and the fourth (and last) very clearly divided into three, with interstadial phases of comparative warmth. Our chronology for Palæolithic man, therefore, can best be given in terms of Glacial or Interglacial periods, without attempting to correlate these with the time-scale in thousands of solar years which has been computed from the solar radiation curve, but which involves such vast stretches of time that the figures become meaningless to the ordinary mind.

The Palæolithic cultures and industries can be divided

conveniently into Lower Palæolithic, covering the earliest
Pleistocene periods up to the Third Interglacial, and
Upper Palæolithic, confined to the Fourth Glacial period
with its two interstadial periods of climatic amelioration:
an elusive Middle Palæolithic which has been claimed,
centred chronologically on the Last Interglacial period,
need not debar us from making this essential twofold
division for the European and British cultures.

It is clear therefore that even the minimum extent
of the permanent ice in glacial times left only southern
Britain as a tiny territory still part of the European land-
mass but on the ultimate edge of possible human habitation. At the end of the Pleistocene, when rather more
stable human communities seem to have been established
than in the earlier ages, an apparently reliable estimate
of the winter population of what is now southern Britain
can be made, and in the earlier periods a figure of
under 200 persons may well be reasonable; but when
viewing the very large collections of English Palæolithic
flint tools, displayed in so many museums, one must
remember that two or three might well have been made
by one man in a day, and that the whole series has to
be spread over a period of hundreds of thousands of
years and could therefore well be the product of small
bands of migratory hunters.

The importance of the Palæolithic phase of human
culture, however, lies in the fact that here, at the end
of the geological sequence of the evolution of vertebrates,
and of the mammals, we see the first emergence of the
tool-using, fire-making, and speaking human species.
Wherever man first developed as a being distinct from
the higher apes, it was not in the Ultima Thule of
Britain, and evidence suggests the possibility that certain

apes, known from Tertiary deposits in Africa and the Siwalik Hills in north-west India, may be pointers to the cradle of human origins in one or both of these regions. To appreciate the Palæolithic cultures of Britain we have to take a world view—or, at least, an Old World view, since the peopling of the American continent seems to have occurred in comparatively late times— and regard the remnants of these very ancient primitive cultures in Britain in the light of the wider distribution of similar types.

The climatic conditions in northern Europe during the glacial periods, where the land surface was free from the huge thickness of the ice-sheet but still within a zone of arctic cold, would be tundra steppe conditions with low scrub at most, and the wild fauna would include bison, reindeer, and the types of long-haired elephant (mammoth) and rhinoceros (woolly rhinoceros) adapted to life under extremely cold conditions. In the Inter-glacial periods, sub-tropical or tropical climates super-vened, with great rivers and areas of marsh resulting from the melting of the ice-sheet, lush vegetation, and the tropical species of elephant, rhinoceros, and hippo-potamus. The enormous geological periods and land-movements involved mean that for the Lower Palæolithic we have no remains of the impermanent camps which would have marked the temporary halting-places of the tribes of a hunting community, but only the debris of their stone tools contained in geological deposits such as the gravels laid down by rivers flowing with greater force and at higher levels than to-day. In ex-ceptionally favoured circumstances in East Africa such Lower Palæolithic hunting camps have in fact been discovered in recent years. The famous Swanscombe skull, of a maker of Lower Palæolithic tools, was found lying in an ancient gravel laid down by an earlier version of the Lower Thames and now fifteen to twenty feet below ground, and it is only in the Upper Palæolithic that we find habitation sites clearly recognizable in Britain, where, as in France, caves were used for winter occupation and have preserved the layers of accumulated debris of recurrent settlements from destruction by natural causes.

The earliest human fossils which can be called ' men ' come from the Far East. Geologically, probably the earliest is from Java, an island famous since the end of the last century for its ' ape-man ' fossil, and since then many additional finds of humans of this species have been made, one of which may belong to the First Interglacial period, thus probably antedating by some millennia the rest of the human fossils (including the original find) which belong to the Second Glacial period. These skeletal remains indicate a type of human classified as *Pithecanthropus erectus* and still retaining ape-like characteristics in the skull, but with limb-bones of more or less modern type indicating that Pithecanthropus walked upright. Closely related to these Java men are those from the now well-known Chou-kou-tien cave near Pekin, originally named as a separate species, *Sinanthropus,* but now regarded by most anatomists as varieties of *Pithecanthropus,* related to the Java race in the same degree as whites, mongoloids, negroes, and australoids are to-day, and it is these Pekin finds, dating from the Second Interglacial, that contain the first evidence in the archæological record of the deliberate use of fire by human beings, for there were remains of hearths in the cave, as well as roughly chipped quartz implements.

No members of the *Pithecanthropus* race are known from England, nor indeed from Europe, though a lower jaw from near Heidelberg, dating from at least the middle of the Second Glacial period, may be a related form or even a descendant. The evidence of the available fossil human skeletons from the Old World suggests that even at the beginning of the Pleistocene there may have been two main human stocks already evolved, one tending to preserve and perpetuate the more simian characteristics of heavy brow-ridges, receding forehead, and undeveloped chin, accompanied with powerful muscular development, and the other containing the elements which make up the physical characteristics of modern man to-day. It is possible, though unproven through the paucity of finds, that the first of these, the Palæoanthropic stem (to which *Pithecanthropus* belongs), may have had an original area of settlement in Asia, while the second, the Neoanthropic group, was characteristic of Africa and Europe.

The extreme antiquity of *Homo sapiens*, and of the Neoanthropic stem to which he belongs, is shown by an English find of outstanding importance, the skull from Swanscombe in Kent, which dates from the Second Interglacial period. The cranial fragments discovered here, in gravels of known geological age and associated with flint implements of a type to be described below, represent a skull indistinguishable in its essentials from those of modern man. The high degree of evolution implied in this find, of Middle Pleistocene age, suggests that the Neoanthropic stock must go back to a remarkably early date, and gives colour to the belief that our human ancestry may go back well into the Pliocene geological period. A well-known English find, the skull found at Piltdown in Sussex many years ago, should give evidence on this, but unfortunately it presents several complex problems. The geological date of the deposit in which the skull fragments were found is not beyond dispute— it is undoubtedly very ancient, and of Pleistocene age, but the evidence which would otherwise tend to place it at the very outset of this geological phase is not conclusive. Again, the skeletal remains from the Pilt- down pit comprise not only cranial fragments of a skull of *Homo sapiens* type, not dissimilar from the Swanscombe skull, but also a lower jaw and canine tooth of decidedly simian form. There is some measure of agreement among anatomists to-day in regarding the cranium as human, and the jaw as that of a large ape, the two being acciden- tally brought together in the deposition of the gravel in which they lay, but the problem can by no means be considered as satisfactorily cleared up, and Piltdown Man (*Eoanthropus dawsoni*) remains one of the most unsatisfactory of the early human fossils.

The remaining finds of fossil men of Pleistocene date in Britain are confined to representatives of the *Homo sapiens* race of Upper Palæolithic times and belonging to the time of the Fourth Glacial period. For our know- ledge of Lower Palæolithic Britain, therefore, we have to turn to man-made tools and other implements, found for the most part in circumstances not directly con- nected with distinctive habitation sites, though occurring in stratified deposits in such a way that a chronological framework can be established into which a typological series of stone tools can be fitted. Here again we must consider the English material in its wider setting, for even in this remote corner of the Lower Palæolithic world we can detect in the human industries tech- nological peculiarities which recur elsewhere in Europe,

Asia, and Africa, and which seem to owe their origins to remote and world-wide cleavages in the evolution of tool-making techniques.

There can be distinguished, when surveying the whole Old World corpus of Lower Palæolithic stone tools, two great 'families' of contrasted traditions in their manufacture, with distinctive geographical distributions. Basically, all such tools must be made by chipping or flaking a piece of stone to the required shape—for the production of a cutting edge, for instance. But this may be done in two ways, either by chipping and flaking a lump until all superfluous material is removed from the central core, which itself becomes the desired implement, or by detaching from the block a large flake of stone and working this up into the finished state. These two techniques, producing 'core' or 'flake' tools respectively, seem in the main to represent quite distinctive cultural traditions, the core - tools being characteristic of the African continent and Europe, with an eastward limit of at least South India, while the flake-tools are essentially Asiatic, spreading over an area from the Far East westwards to Europe, where they overlap with those in core technique. These contrasted distributions are suggestive, though not decisive, of some correlation between techniques and human types; between flake-tools and the Palæoanthropic group, and core-tools and the Neoanthropic stem. We shall see that some evidence from England helps to strengthen this supposition in part, and it is important to realize that divergent tool-making techniques, artificial and unimportant as they may seem to us to-day, do in the intense conservatism of primitive workmanship have a real cultural significance.

The life and social structure of Lower Palæolithic communities are so imperfectly known to us because we have only a fraction of the evidence of the material culture preserved; the durability of stone tools has given them an artificial survival-value which may well be disproportionate in the life of the tribe who used them in Pleistocene times. The whole perishable element in personal or tribal possessions has irrecoverably vanished, and we must be grateful even for chipped flints as a record of Pleistocene man's existence. It is salutary to turn in parenthesis to modern primitives in a comparable stage of cultural evolution, such as the northern Australian hunting tribes. To take a single instance, the Wik Monkan tribe in Queensland have a complicated social structure of patrilineal clans, and follow an elaborate annual cycle of activities in their food-quest by hunting or food-gathering. In these activities, which entail a largely nomadic existence, they use bark canoes, fish-nets, fish-traps and weirs made of wood and basketry; fish-hooks, harpoons, hunting spears of wood, sometimes with bone tips; digging-sticks for roots, a variety of baskets and bark vessels; they make half a dozen or more types of wooden structures for houses, food-stores, and other purposes. Of this well-organized and flourishing savage community, nothing would survive for the archæologist except a few ambiguous pieces of sharpened bone and worked shell—and the latter only a borrowing from neighbouring coastal dwellers!

We must therefore constantly bear in mind the incomplete nature of the evidence for the life of Lower Palæolithic man: such incompleteness, as we have seen, is inherent in the whole archæological record, but more striking in the most ancient phases. In default of material on which to base any reconstruction of Lower Palæolithic society, and of its hunting and food-gathering techniques, we must turn, however reluctantly, to the typology of the stone tools and their geological stratification for at least some outline of the distribution in time and space of the various main human groups (possibly ethnic, certainly cultural) as reflected in their tool-making techniques.

There is some not wholly incontrovertible evidence which implies that recognizable man-made tools in England may go back in geological time to the very end of the Pliocene period, immediately before the First Glacial period which ushers in the Pleistocene. In the past there has been much debate about these and similar tools, sometimes referred to as 'Eoliths', from early Pleistocene or earlier deposits. In certain East Anglian deposits, notably in the neighbourhood of Cromer, Norwich, and Ipswich, a certain percentage of broken flints seem the products of human handiwork: very massive flake-tools at Cromer, and elsewhere a curious form known as a rostro-carinate implement, which might claim a place in the hypothetical ancestry of core-tools. But it is not until the First Interglacial that we can claim quite undoubted human artifacts, concerning which neither the archæology nor the geology can be called into question.

At this point in geological time we find the earliest representatives of the core-tool family, a class of pear-shaped implements usually known (rather unsatisfactorily) as 'hand-axes', and of frankly unknown use, except in so far as they could be used for various unspecialized purposes of cutting and hacking, and probably also for grubbing up edible roots. A progressive mastery over the technique of stone-flaking (in England almost invariably flint, the most satisfactory substance for this purpose) can be traced, the typological series being in accordance with the relative geological sequence of the changing styles, the whole series being spread over a vast epoch of time with relatively little modification in the essential hand-axe type save a progressive refinement of technique. Spatially, too, parallel evolution of the type can be observed over huge areas, whether in Europe or in South and East Africa.

The earliest forms of hand-axe, grouped as Abbevillian, in England as in France, from the site at Abbeville near Amiens, following the practice of type-site nomenclature usual in prehistory, have strong, irregular flaking which experiment has shown to be the product of striking with stone rather than any more resilient substance. By the end of the First Interglacial the flaking style was refining, and the beginnings of the long hand-axe tradition known as Acheulean were established: a tradition which endured with modifications until well into the Third Interglacial in Europe and Britain. In these implements the flaking becomes shallow and accomplished, showing the use of a wood or horn baton for striking, giving added resilience to the blow, and the implements show a tendency to become smaller.

What these developments mean in terms of human culture we do not know. The persistence of the type must mean continuity of tradition, conservatism to a fantastic degree, and a poverty of invention; all features which might well be imposed on small human communities by the hard conditions of hunting and food-gathering in the tropical forests of the Great Interglacial, when the Acheulean culture is best represented. To this middle phase belongs the skull of the earliest *Homo sapiens* from the Swanscombe gravels, found in association with Acheulean implements—significant perhaps of the relationship between the Neoanthropic human stock and the manufacture of core-tools.

Side by side with the Abbevillian core-tools of the First Interglacial there is evidence that tribes working in the flake-tool tradition were already established in northern Europe. A distinctive series of such tools, which technological considerations suggest were struck off with hammer-stones from a flint block held against another, which functioned as an anvil, has been named Clactonian from their East Anglian finding-place, and their range in time continues into the Great Interglacial.

The Clactonian industries with various modifications of technique run, as we have seen, parallel with the core technique of the Acheulean, and there is another flake industry, perhaps a distinctive technique of flint-flaking rather than a representative of a separate human group, named from the French site of Levallois and ranging in time from the Second Interglacial up into the Fourth Glacial period. The very characteristic flake-tool industry known as the Mousterian, and associated in Europe and Asia with skeletal remains of the last representative of the Palæoanthropic stock to survive, *Homo neanderthalensis*, is hardly present in England except for a retarded and late occurrence in the Upper Palæolithic at one or two sites. Neanderthal Man—the beetle-browed, shallow-jawed ' Cave Man ' of popular humour—represents a very interesting descendant of the Palæoanthropic group that retained the more simian characteristics as seen for instance in *Pithecanthropus*, and ranges in geological time from the

Third Interglacial into the first phase of the Fourth Glacial period, when the race appears to have died out. There is evidence, however, to suggest that there is an appreciable Neanderthal contribution to the *sapiens* race of the Upper Palæolithic (and therefore ultimately in our own blood), either by interbreeding between Palæoanthropic and Neoanthropic races, or by an evolutionary process out of certain Neanderthal types as known for instance in Palestine. No human remains of *Homo neanderthalensis* are known from England, though they have been found as near as Jersey—a proximity still more marked in the absence of the English Channel in Pleistocene times.

Apart from the stone tools, which have survived in large numbers in southern England, very little evidence of work in other substances has survived, though a piece of mammoth bone found with the Piltdown skull was believed to have been shaped by man, and the tip of a wooden spear, sharpened and hardened by fire, was found with the early flake industry at Clacton, preserved by a lucky accident of mineralization.

Behind this array of stone tools, which it must be confessed are not very inspiring except to the specialist, we can trace the pattern of life of these first stone-using men in England—members of small family or tribal units dependent on the herds of animals they hunted for their sustenance, and with no more economic stability than the capacity of making a fire and a windbreak could confer. Deadfalls and pits may well have been used to trap the larger game, but decisive evidence at this period is lacking: the spear was known, though not it seems the bow, and the club is certainly likely to have been used for various purposes, including killing the larger fish in shallow water, which could also be trapped seasonally in rough dams across the streams. We have already commented on the virtual certainty of a very small migratory population, and the average expectation of life cannot have been high: of the known Neanderthal individuals from Europe, 55 per cent. had died before the age of twenty-one, and only 20 per cent. reached thirty.

At the time of the onset of the Fourth Glaciation the core-tool cultures characterized by ' hand-axes ' seem to have died out in Europe, and specialized flake industries, which, as we have seen, are associated with the Palæoanthropic race of *Homo neanderthalensis*, dominate the archæological record from Russian Turkestan to western France. Then comes evidence of folk-movements —migrations and treks which seem more purposeful than the casual wandering of hunting tribes following their quarry—and these movements are associated with *Homo sapiens*, now distinctively developed as the culmination of the Neoanthropic evolution, and indistinguishable from modern races of men to-day. The end of Neanderthal man is wholly obscure in its causes and its manner, but the fossil record is unambiguous. The Upper Palæolithic cultures ushered in with the final glacial period are the new, distinctive products of modern man, arriving in north-western Europe as an immigrant from elsewhere, and in some manner supplanting the last remnants of the Palæoanthropic race that may have had its origins in the Pithecanthropoid types of the Second Glaciation.

The evidence strongly suggests that these new hunting groups in Europe and Britain ultimately came from the Near East in three main migrations: an early move seems to have included North and East Africa as well as Europe in its sphere of colonization; another may have originated in Persia, spreading thence through the Caucasus and the shores of the Black Sea westwards; and the third, early established in Kurdistan, later reached south Russia and eventually western Europe. The two latter at least reached that part of southern England free from ice, and forming the north-western fringe of habitable Europe before the formation of the English Channel.

The economy of these cultures was, as in the Lower Palæolithic, centred round the means of food production —the hunting of wild animals by all the wiles of stalking or trapping, with some ancillary food-gathering of roots and berries. But more evidence is available in the archæological record (though not a great deal in England). The detailed economy of Upper Palæolithic mammoth hunters, for instance, can be studied in Russia and Central Europe, that of horse and reindeer hunters in France and Germany, and from these we can interpret the rather scanty English material. The need for adequate winter dwellings in the arctic or sub-arctic conditions of the last glaciation called for the provision of warm shelter of some kind, and the problem was solved in Russia and probably in Central Europe too by building semi-subterranean houses, roofed over with earth and sods carried on mammoth-bone rafters. But in France and in Britain winter shelter was found in natural caves in limestone and similar rocks, and it is from the accumulated domestic debris which piled up in the mouths of such caves that we can recover something of the outline at least of their ancient history as human habitations.

Such use of caves had already been made by Neanderthal man, and it is with remains of these primitive humans in France, Palestine, and the Crimea that we find the first evidence in the archæological record of the conception of deliberate burial of the dead, and with deposits of meat and possibly implements by the side of the corpse, which can only indicate belief in some sort of an after-life. In England, the stone tools of the Mousterian type usually associated with Neanderthal man have been found in caves such as Kent's Cavern near Torquay, and Creswell Crags in Derbyshire, but their actual date seems later than their type alone would suggest, and they may represent either retarded survivals of technique or possibly they were made by emigrants from France after the arrival of the new Upper Palæolithic tribes. Associated with such stone tools in one Derbyshire cave was a small oval bone tablet, perforated at one end, which is believed to be an example of the mystic object known as a ' bull-roarer ', which, whirled round on the end of a string, produces the roaring, whistling sound that is the voice of God to the Australian blackfellow, and which is regarded with some awe and much superstition in the many simple cultures where it is used, half as a toy, up to the present day. The Derbyshire object, if rightly interpreted, would take this curious religious idea well back into the Upper Palæolithic.

The cultures associated with *Homo sapiens*, and intrusive to the previous sequence of European Palæolithic techniques, are characterized by the use of various forms of small flint tools made on finely flaked blades, and by an increasing use of bone and antler. On the typology of these tools, checked against the stratigraphy of occupation deposits in caves and other habitation sites, a

sequence of Upper Palæolithic cultures has been worked
out in great detail for France, and this sequence can
be applied with modification to England, but it is
important to remember that specialized tool types may
be dictated by the particular nature of the community's
food-quest. It is clear that mammoth hunters might use
a very different equipment for the chase from that of a
tribe who hunted reindeer, and it is at least possible
that some of the ' cultural ' distinctions that have been
made by archæologists really denote varying hunting
traditions.

In that part of England left habitable in glacial
conditions, some eighteen to twenty caves have been
identified in such areas as Devonshire, West Wales, the
Mendips, and Derbyshire, as having served as winter
shelters to Upper Palæolithic families. Though the ' cave-
man ' is popularly confined to the Palæolithic period,
it is interesting to notice that living in caves, at least
intermittently, is a common and recurrent feature of
life in prehistoric Britain, and the statistics of finds
indicate that the maximum period of cave occupation
was not in the Palæolithic at all, but during the Roman
Occupation. Animals had shown the way—the hyænas
in a cave at Wookey in the Mendips had established
themselves so well during the Fourth Glacial period
that the gnawed and broken skeletal debris of the prey
they had dragged in was found by the modern excavators in heaps totalling many thousand bones: one
season's work produced evidence of sixteen species of
wild animal, among which may be noted bones indicating four hundred wild horses, thirty mammoths and a
like number of bison, reindeer, giant elk, and cave bear,
and over two hundred representatives of the woolly.

rhinoceros. These figures give some indication of the vast natural resources of animal flesh available to the small bands of Palæolithic hunters on the tundras of what is now Somerset.

In none of the caves, however, does there seem to have been more than seasonal occupation, and that not of very great intensity. It seems likely that we have identified almost all the available caves which might have been suitable for Palæolithic occupation, and as the settlement debris in these does not suggest large groups of persons dwelling there, a reasonable estimate has been made of the Upper Palæolithic population of habitable England as about 250 persons—four or five bus-loads in a London street.

The Upper Palæolithic physical type, known from a large number of skeletons in Europe and some from England, was in general tall, long-limbed, and slender, and not excessively robust. The hands and feet were large, the hips narrow, and the shoulders broad, and so far as one can equate skeletal forms between living and extinct types of men, it is suggested that some groups at least may have resembled the North American Plains Indian, though the pigmentation of the ancient type is of course unknown. In his physical make-up Upper Palæolithic *Homo sapiens* seems to have included elements from both the Palæoanthropic and the Neo-anthropic stems, and of the former contribution, to quote a recent study, we cannot assume that it was ' less intelligent or, in the social and intellectual sense, less human than the original *sapiens* species '.

In terms of the cultural divisions of the Upper Palæo-lithic to which reference has been made, we can trace in the English material evidence of at least the second

D

(Aurignacian) and third (Gravettian) move of peoples
from the Orient to Europe, and there are slight traces of
a culture (the Solutrean) which may have originated in
north-west Africa or south Spain and seems to have been
largely centred on hunting wild horses. A specific French
development, following stratigraphically (and so chronologically) on this in the European sequence, and basically
concerned with reindeer-hunting, is named the Magda-
lenian, and again shows some evidence of having extended
to England; or, at least, some of its characteristic barbed
bone or antler spear-points were acquired by trade or
interchange to turn up in the occupational debris of
the English caves. These subdivisions are named from
French sites: Aurignac, La Gravette, Solutré, La
Madeleine.

The Gravettian culture seems, however, to have taken
firmest root in England, and in the Derbyshire caves a
distinctive insular development of this can be seen
taking place at the end of the Fourth Glacial period,
producing flint implements of a type known from the
caves at Creswell Crags as the Creswellian culture. By
the time this development was taking place, however, the
fourth and last glaciation was coming to a close, and
we shall meet the Creswellian again with the oncoming
of a new series of climatic modifications leading up to
those of to-day. In the meantime we may review in
outline the material, and something of the spiritual
culture, of the Upper Palæolithic cultures of Britain as
a whole.

The material remains of these people in England consist
of a not very impressive collection of flint implements
including various forms of skin-dressing scrapers, awls,
gravers for cutting bone and leather, and single-edged

blades which are the ancestors of the whole family of knives as we know them to-day. There is evidence of the use of the bow as well as the spear. Bone and mammoth ivory were carved into points (which might be used for netting, or as gorges on a fishing line), barbed spear-points (' harpoons '), bangles (from the hollow base of a mammoth tusk), and curious perforated and sometimes decorated rods which might have served the utilitarian purpose of straightening arrow-shafts (on modern Eskimo analogies), or may perhaps rather have had some symbolic meaning as wands of authority. In the French caves the best-known feature of the Upper Palæolithic is of course the naturalistic art, represented by paintings on the cave walls with charcoal, ochre, and other colours mixed with fat, and by numerous small objects carved or engraved in bone and ivory. This exceedingly brilliant artistic output is for all its technical ability essentially that of primitive peoples who can form direct mental links only between an object and a photographic rendering of it—the cave paintings are true ' snapshots ' of animals imagined on to the walls with the vivid force possessed to-day only by persons psychologically classed as eidetics, and represented by an assured technique which sometimes descends from real brilliance to the slick formula of a modern commercial artist. The appreciation of the picture as a symbol, which leads in later prehistoric periods to completely non-representational art, involves a greater complexity of mental processes, and probably also of speech images, than Upper Palæolithic man appears to have possessed.

But above all, the function of Palæolithic art was utilitarian, and designed to increase or secure by magic the beasts of the chase that were portrayed. There is dramatic evidence of this from France, where spear-marks can be seen on the painted animals or dinting the clay figure originally covered by a bear-skin, and in England there is one tiny but very significant find which is almost our only example of Upper Palæolithic art, an engraved bone from Creswell Crags in Derby-shire. On this is roughly scratched a little, phallic, human figure holding a bow, and wearing an animal's mask over his head. He is cousin to the great painting of the 'sorcerer' in Ariège, similarly disguised as a fantastic animal, and in these most ancient concepts of the man disguised as a beast for magic rites we see the beginning of a tradition in pagan Europe surviving until the Penitentials of the seventh century A.D. denounced the abominable heathen custom of disguising oneself as a bull-calf on the Kalends of January, and represented even to-day in the arty-crafty innocence of the Abbots Bromley Horn Dance.

Not only was Upper Palæolithic man's mind con-cerned with the irrationalities of mimetic magic and a superstitious belief in unseen powers controlling his seemingly inconsequent universe. The ritual of the burial of the dead had already taken on the importance it was to occupy throughout prehistoric times, and the belief in a future life to which archæologists owe eternal gratitude, involving as it did the deposition of material objects for use in an immaterial underworld by the dead man's ghost, had clearly become an established part of man's set of spiritual assumptions. An important Upper Palæolithic burial in England shows this very well. In the Paviland Cave in the Gower Peninsula of South Wales the burial of a young man, belonging to the phase of the Palæolithic designated Aurignacian (ultimately of Near Eastern derivation, as we have seen), was found in a grave dug into the debris on the cave floor, and with a large boulder set at head and foot in the manner of grave-stones. The corpse had been thickly coated with red ochre before burial, in a pathetic attempt to bring back the ruddy colouring of life to the dead flesh, and with the dead man had been placed various offerings—a handful of periwinkles, bored teeth and shell beads, ivory awls and an ivory bangle—and near by was a mammoth skull which seems to have been placed as an offering of food. Funeral ritual had clearly been firmly established, and perhaps the priest or magician or medicine-man can be claimed as the first specialized craftsman in human societies.

The retreat of the ice-sheet at the close of the Fourth Glacial period was, like the previous climatic changes of the Pleistocene geological period, a slow process stretching over millennia. But its effects were decisive in causing the end of steppe and tundra conditions in northern Europe, and with the changing landscape and vegetation went the retreat of the herds of reindeer, wild horses, and other beasts that had formed the main quarry of the Upper Palæolithic hunters, but which now sought open lands farther and farther to the north as the formerly unforested areas began to be covered with trees. The succession of forest history in northern Europe has been worked out in some detail by palæo-botanists, largely on the evidence of the pollen contained in peat-bogs, blown in by the wind from adjacent forest areas, and while it is probably dangerous to make exact correlations between, for instance, Denmark and Ireland, and even sometimes within the British Isles themselves, there is no doubt about the main sequence of climatic (and consequently vegetational) phases, which form a useful framework against which the human cultures can be set.

The initial climatic phase with which we are concerned here, the Boreal, followed a stage when sparse birch, aspen, and willow began to clothe the former steppe-lands, and is marked by the appearance of pine forests and a rather drier climate than at present. This is succeeded by the Atlantic phase, with moister, more maritime climate and a spread of woods including alder and essentially dominated by oaks. We shall see reason for believing that the Atlantic phase was coming to an end by about 2000 B.C., to be followed by slightly drier and warmer conditions in the Sub-Boreal, which had again deteriorated in the Sub-Atlantic phase to the cold and wet conditions in which we still continue to-day, by about 500 B.C. Concurrently, and linked, with these climatic changes were land movements, or at least sea incursions into the European coastline. In Boreal times the North Sea was still an area of pine woods, though doubtless with much fresh-water marsh and widespread lagoons. By Atlantic times the same area was sea-covered, while the separation of Britain from the European continent by the formation of the English Channel seems to have taken place as early as about 6000 B.C. Lesser changes in the coastline continued to take place, as we shall see, at the beginning of the first millennium B.C. and later, resulting in the submergence of considerable areas in southern England from the East Anglian fens to the Scilly Islands. On the other hand, there was a rise of the land in the north, so that sea-beaches came to be left high and dry beyond the present shore-line in many areas of Scotland and northern Ireland.

These natural changes forced upon the descendants of the Upper Palæolithic hunters the necessity of modifying their technique of living and food-securing. Smaller game than that which had formed the great herds of the past had now to be hunted in scrub and woodland, there were wild fowl and fish to be caught in the marshes and along the rivers, and shell-fish to be collected on the shores. The forests too presented a challenge which was taken up, and stone tools were evolved for the first time deliberately designed for cutting down trees—the axe, which in prehistoric northern Europe was as much a symbol of the battle of man with the natural environment as it was with the nineteenth - century pioneers in North America.

This period of adaptation to the post-glacial environment of northern Europe is conveniently known as the Mesolithic (Middle Stone Age), and under this term are comprised a number of more or less distinct cultures sharing the same hunting and food-gathering economy, but with a major distinction into two groups. One group, centred on the Baltic and comprising what are sometimes known as the Forest Cultures, is distinguished by the use of various forms of flint and stone axes for tree-felling, a form of what is technically called a ' heavy stone industry ' not known among the other groups. In Britain we see the interaction of at least three groups of Mesolithic cultures in Boreal and early Atlantic times, and the continental affinities of the three groups no less than their points of primary colonization in Britain form a pattern which we shall see recurring throughout the whole of prehistory.

The existence of large tracts of dry land, interspersed by easily navigable fens, over the area of what is now the North Sea, resulted in south-east England being in effect a westerly province of the Forest Cultures of Scandinavia, characterized by the use of the flint axe and of distinctive barbed bone points for fish-spears and similar hunting weapons. The area of settlement extended up the coastal fringe at least to Northumberland, and was, as might be expected, well established in East Anglia, but its western limits are less well defined since it overlaps with another group of immigrant colonists, contributing to their range of stone implements the distinctive axe. This second group of British Mesolithic cultures has strong affinities in the types of its flint implements with certain north French and Belgian communities, and two successive moves of immigrants can be detected for the same continental homeland. These people can be traced not only abundantly in south-eastern England, but spreading westwards to the Welsh coasts and in central England to the Pennines, where there is evidence also of survival, in the Peak District, of Upper Palæolithic cultures into post-glacial times. These immigrants, bearers of what is known as the Tardenoisian culture of the Mesolithic (from La Fère-en-Tardenois in north France), seem to have arrived after the formation of the English Channel, which they must have crossed in some form of boats, while the third group of Mesolithic colonists certainly made considerable sea-voyages by coasting up the Irish Sea. Small communities established in the west Scottish islands such as Colonsay and Oronsay and on the mainland coast—grouped as the Obanian culture, from caves at Oban—have left their remains in heaps of shells resulting from countless successive seasons of beachcombing, and their tool-types, particularly their barbed fish-spears, connect them without much doubt with the Azilian group of Mesolithic folk in south France (named from Mas d'Azil in Ariège). These Scottish settlements again seem to have come in contact with the northerly outposts of the east-coast Forest folk, whose tools have been found with the skeletons of stranded whales in the Firth of Forth.

The settlement pattern of Mesolithic Britain was therefore that of three main interrelated cultures having their ultimate origins in Scandinavia, Belgium, and south France respectively. The population must have been small, but it must also have been largely immigrant in the earlier phase, for the aboriginal descendants of the Upper Palæolithic folk, responsible for the Creswellian culture, are not likely to have been numerous nor established save in a few localities. Communities of Forest folk related to those named from the Danish site of Maglemose were established in southeastern England in Boreal times, and some of the Tardenoisian settlements of Belgian derivation had taken place before the formation of peat of Atlantic age; but the Obanian coastal settlements in west Scotland seem all to be late Atlantic in date. The economy thus established had a very long persistence, and, as we shall see, there is reason to think that the ultimate descendants of the Mesolithic hunting and fishing peoples formed a very important element at the end of the Neolithic and beginning of the Early Bronze Age.

Remains of the culture of Maglemosean affinities in east England are scanty but distinctive, and not least interesting is the barbed bone prong from a fish-spear dredged up from the Leman and Ower Bank in the North Sea, embedded in fresh-water peat of Boreal age, and doubtless lost by a Mesolithic hunter in what was then a fresh-water mere among pine woods. Other spear-points have been found in eastern England, and decorated pieces of antler or bone, while chipped flint axes are evidence of the beginnings of tree-cutting and carpentry. Canoes hollowed out from complete tree trunks may be of Mesolithic date in Scotland, and in north Europe wooden paddles and actual remains of nets with bark floats give more substance to the picture of the riverine fisher-folk which the Maglemoseans must have been. In Surrey at Farnham, and Sussex at Selmeston, the mixed culture resulting in a fusion of Tardenoisians and Forest folk is represented by more than one camp site or small village. The huts were partly scooped into the ground to a depth of about three feet, and were of roughly oval plan, ranging from about 30 by 15 feet to 15 by 8 feet, and having in all probability a lean-to roof open on one side, where the supporting post could be traced in one instance as a socket cut in the ground for its reception. These huts are comparable to the Upper Palæolithic winter houses already referred to, known from Russia, and both may be compared to Eskimo types of dwelling and probably represent Mesolithic winter camps, one at least of which was situated near a particularly good spring.

The Tardenoisian folk have left little in the archæological record save a mass of tiny flint tools, probably used in wooden hafts to form composite fish-spears or bird-arrows, but in the Pennines, at an altitude of over a thousand feet, traces of what must be summer camps have been found, probably of Boreal age, with indications of small, light, semicircular shelters, and similar traces have been found in the Isle of Man.

These shelters suggest the huts of the Tasmanian aborigines, which sheltered three or four persons only and were never in groups of more than about four. From a Tardenoisian site in Pembrokeshire comes a collection of tiny disc beads and a probable pendant, and perforated shells forming a necklace were found in Oronsay —about the only evidence from Britain of the personal adornment of these folk.

The settlements of the Obanian folk on the shores of Oronsay comprise a vast quantity of discarded shells of edible molluscs and animal and bird bones, enabling us to appreciate something of the diet, and of the fishing and hunting activities, of the Mesolithic settlers in the southern Hebrides. The red deer and wild boar are the only land animals represented, but two species of seal and the otter occur. The dozen or so species of birds include, as might be expected, cormorants, gulls, gannets, guillemots, razor-bills, and the now extinct Great Auk; fish comprised eight species, among which conger eel, bream, wrasse, haddock, and dogfish appear. The huge accumulations of shells were of over two dozen species of mollusc, the more familiar being limpet, whelk, winkle, mussel, oyster (the deep-sea variety), cockle, and scallop.

Dug into the accumulating midden debris, and later to be covered by successive deposits, were the post-holes of a large semicircular windbreak about 24 feet across and supported on six posts, and among the debris here and at other sites of the Obanian culture were found the bone and antler double-barbed harpoons or fish-spears of types clearly related to those used by Mesolithic people of the Azilian culture in Ariège. It is a remarkable fact that no intermediate coastal settlements have been traced between France and south-west Scotland, but we shall encounter an almost parallel phenomenon when we trace in a later chapter the spread of certain types of collective stone-built tombs in the Neolithic period. In both instances the long-distance sea-journey, however broken by frequent landing and hardly out of sight of the coast for more than a few hours at any point, is a most outstanding achievement.

Within Britain, there was considerable interchange of ideas, technique, and probably population. The flint-axe tradition spread from the region of primary Magle-mose colonization across to the west coasts, in Wales and southern Scotland, and even some of the Oronsay harpoons show modifications on the original Azilian model which strongly suggests Forest folk influence, while an Obanian bone harpoon from the Durham coast shows that a west-to-east route was also followed. It is probably in the movements of these lightly equipped, mobile hunting folk through the forests and across the moors of Britain in the early Atlantic phase that we should look for the origins of the routes which in later prehistoric periods become clearly defined as those of traders, especially those engaged in the distribution of early metal objects and ores from west Britain and Ireland to the richer agricultural lands of the south and south-east.

CHAPTER III

THE NEOLITHIC PERIOD

WITH the coming of the Atlantic climatic phase in Europe, at a date which may reasonably be computed to be about 5000 B.C., we are able to consider the British Isles with the coastlines familiar to us to-day, and under conditions of vegetation and physical geography which, though powerfully modified by the past four thousand years of agriculture and rural exploitation, are nevertheless more recognizable and comprehensible than the steppes and tundras of the North European plain in the last phases of the Ice Ages. The formation of the English Channel, severing England from the continental landmass, seems to have taken place in late Boreal times, about 6000 B.C., and though the detail of the coastline was to undergo some further variations at the beginning of the second millennium B.C., the main features of the map of Britain were already fixed before that date.

In studying the human occupation of the islands in prehistoric times we have constantly to be aware of the natural pattern of mountain and moorland, fenland and river valley, upon which all distributions of man by settlement or burial, and across which all movements of migration or trade, were necessarily imposed. Much remains to-day as a witness of the extreme variety of British geography within a small area—the chalk uplands of Wessex or Lincolnshire, the high moorland of Wales or Scotland, the limestone escarpments of the Cotswolds or of Sligo, the dead level of the Cambridgeshire

fens, and the heavy clay lands of the Midland shires
are still inescapable reminders of the structural distinctions of British topography despite the ploughing,
the road-making, the railway construction, and the
town-building, which has tended to efface these regional
variants in soil and vegetation. But before an agricultural
economy had forced on man the necessity for forest
clearance and cultivation of crops (and for many centuries while such exploitation was relatively ineffective
save in small, isolated areas), the physical structure of
Britain, and the vegetation which was the natural
product of the varying subsoils, forms a background to
human endeavour in these islands that should never be
forgotten.

The position of Britain in relation to the continental
land-mass renders it accessible by sea-routes from three
main regions: from the Atlantic coasts of Spain, Portugal,
and west France; from the French coast of the Channel;
and from the lands forming the southern and eastern
boundaries of the North Sea. We have seen these lines
of approach already foreshadowed in the distribution of
mesolithic settlements, and we shall see them recurring
throughout British prehistory, and through historical
times up to the invasion threats of recent years. The
land which faces the Continent on south and east is
lowland, and in the main a potentially rich agricultural
region, but westwards and northwards lie the moors
and rocks of Dartmoor and Cornwall, the Welsh mountains, the Pennines, with beyond them the predominantly
mountainous country of Northumberland, the Lake
District, and Scotland. The irregular boundary line
between these two great natural divisions of Britain is
the eastern edge of the outcrop of the ancient rocks:

the divisions are the Highland and the Lowland Zones. The invasion coast is that of the Lowland Zone, and to the natural ports and harbourages along its length successive immigrant moves of people from the Continent have come, each tending to impose its alien culture on the communities already in occupation. But the force of invasion, or of the more peaceable spread of new peoples by land-routes over Britain, naturally becomes spent as the hard lands of the Highland Zone are reached—here cultures tend to be absorbed, often appearing with strange local modifications centuries after their establishment, and even their extinction, in the Lowland areas.

But the Highland Zone, it must always be remembered, has a long coastline of its own, providing any number of ports that may serve as ' back doors ' to the region served by the western sea-routes. Along these routes, immigrant bands may arrive in the Highland Zone before their eventual penetration into the Lowlands: it is probably because the Atlantic coasts of the Continent after the end of the third millennium B.C. ceased to be the jumping-off place of new and vigorous cultures that the British Highland Zone tends to be so often in the rear, rather than in the van, of development. But here again was a local circumstance to offset stagnation, for the ores of copper, tin, and gold lie in the ancient Highland rocks of west Britain and Eire, and during the Bronze Age the need of these metals kept a healthy stream of trade flowing towards the Lowland Zone, though the subsequent development of iron as the essential metal for tools eventually enabled such areas as the Forest of Dean, Northamptonshire, and the Sussex Weald to regain for the Lowlands economic self-sufficiency once more, as in the hey-day of the flint axe mined from the chalk.

Within these broad divisions there are noticeable local regions where the Highland-Lowland relationship can be seen operating over an area of a relatively few square miles, but the essential factors governing human settlement in all regions seem to have been the distribution of land too high and too barren to farm, or similarly rendered useless to the agriculturalist by marsh and by the tangled, mixed-oak forest that flourishes on the heavy clay. The English Midlands are over large areas a virtual blank in the archæological record, not from imperfect archæological investigation, but because no effective penetration of their heavy forest was made until the early historic period—the lightly wooded chalk or gravels, easily cleared and tilled, supported a population relatively dense by prehistoric standards. Rivers could be used as highways of movement by dug-out canoe or coracle, but they and stagnant marshes could be equally barriers and even more deadly menaces. Malaria was after all endemic in the Fens until the last century, and the effect on stock-breeders of such devastating parasites as the liver-fluke, which afflict sheep and pass part of their life-cycle in wet conditions, must be borne in mind.

It is therefore against a landscape of virgin forest, peat-covered moorland, bare rocks, and undrained river valleys that we can set the coming of the first agriculturalists to Britain; the cultural groups whose economy is based on the cultivation of grain crops, the domestication of animals, and a more settled existence in village groups than the wandering bands of hunters of palæolithic and mesolithic times. Such a revolution in the technique of living implies a fairly long antecedent period of experiment and adjustment: new technical processes such as pottery-making have to be mastered, and the evolution of domesticated out of wild breeds of animals and plants is a lengthy procedure. A local evolution in northern Europe is therefore, on the face of it, hardly likely, especially as the ancestral wild species of grain, or of cattle and sheep, are unknown in northerly latitudes, and the intrusive character of the neolithic cultures in Britain is in agreement with other European regions, where the old hunting economies are decisively interrupted by the arrival of agriculturalists from outside.

The origins of these stone-using, agricultural economies usually classed as ' neolithic ' can be traced back over the European continent to the Ancient East. In such areas as Palestine, Egypt, Mesopotamia, and Persia there is archæological evidence of agricultural communities living in more or less permanent villages at a very early date which may well be in the neighbourhood of 6000 B.C. It is in these regions that the wild grasses ancestral to our wheat, barley, millet, and other grains grow naturally; here, too, animals such as the sheep have their undomesticated representatives. In Palestine there are cultures which seem to show the very beginnings of the change from hunting to growing grain (or at least reaping a cereal crop which may have been wild or cultivated), though as yet without domesticated animals except the hunter's dog, already tamed even in the northern mesolithic cultures. In northern Iraq a very early agricultural settlement seems to have had no more than temporary shelters or camps, though the ground was being tilled with hoes for a grain crop, and pottery was made: the same site shows a later stage with good, mud-built cottages and evidence of hoe-cultivation, reaping, grain storage, and excellent pottery-making. Much the same sequence can be observed elsewhere in the Orient, and here the relatively rapid development of the small villages into urban communities, using metal tools and with a written system of language, can be studied, so that by 3000 B.C. we pass from prehistory to literacy and the founding of the historical dynasties of Sumer and Egypt, with written records of commerce and of the court and an imaginative literature in poetry and prose.

Beyond these centres of higher civilization we can trace the gradual spread of the simpler concepts of agriculture, and of the settled life of the farmer and the merchant among the old hunting and food-gathering tribes, descendants of the immemorial palæolithic tradition. Such a spread was effected partly by the actual movements of peoples trading or colonizing, partly by the acquisition of new ideas by tribes adjacent to trade routes or marts: the process was slow, and in direct proportion to the distance or geographical inaccessibility of a region from the oriental nuclei. In the European area, we can trace the spread of new ideas and peoples by three main routes—two overland, and one by sea.

The first, and most widely diffused in its routes, was across the great plains and steppes from south Russia to the Baltic, where the mesolithic peasantry acquired the rudiments of pot-making and simple agriculture by a slow process, later accelerated by the movement of small warlike bands over the area. The great natural highway into continental Europe was, however, by way of the

Danube, reached by a route from the Ægean, through the Balkans, along the valleys of the Vardar and Morava rivers to a point near Belgrade, and thence up the great river valley into Germany and beyond. The third route, or group of routes, went by coasting sea-voyages westwards along the Mediterranean and thence overland into France or by farther western sea-routes round the Iberian Peninsula.

Of these three main routes of neolithic colonization, with their resultant cultural provinces in Europe, we have in Britain evidence of the first and the last, for it is in these islands that these very divergent cultural strains meet, the ' Western ' neolithic communities using the sea-ways near the north-easterly limit of their influence, and the ' Nordic ' steppe cultures turning westwards from Scandinavia to Britain, there to contribute in no small degree to the subsequent cultural pattern of our neolithic and Bronze Age settlements.

It is convenient to turn first to the Western neolithic cultures, in which again subdivisions can be observed in their areas of colonization in Britain. At a date probably about 2600 B.C. simple agricultural communities were being established in Spain and southern France, and from the latter region a spread northwards can be traced, partly up the Rhône and partly across the limestone country towards Brittany, the archæological evidence being particularly centred on characteristic pottery bowls of dark leathery ware, round-bottomed and often with paired lug-handles. From points on the French seaboard of the Channel eastward of Brittany there were emigrations of a certain number of these tribes by boat, across to the chalk lands of Wessex and Sussex, probably not more than three or four generations later than the formation of the south French colonies.

Soon after 2500 B.C., therefore, we have the first agricultural settlements established in southern England. Their known distribution extends from Devonshire to Sussex: regional differences in pottery styles suggest several interrelated tribes making direct cross-channel journeys to a number of separate landfalls on the English coast rather than concentration on one port of entry. The area of primary settlement seems to have extended northward at least to the chalk escarpment overlooking the Vale of the White Horse and probably to the middle Thames, and the culture as a whole is named from a site in north Wiltshire, Windmill Hill near Avebury.

The Windmill Hill culture is characterized by certain distinctive types of pottery and stone implements, by evidence of grain-growing and stock-breeding, and by three forms of constructional activity that still remain as visible evidence in the English countryside of the work of these first farmers. These three types of structures reflect the life of the people in as many important aspects—they are earthwork enclosures for seasonal use in cattle-herding, mine-shafts dug into the chalk to extract flint for making axes (an incipient specialized industry), and impressive long mounds covering their burials. At present we have not identified the actual villages of these people, though small settlements of not more than a family have been found, and in Devonshire the foundations of an oblong timber-built house on stone footings has been excavated, about 20 by 12 feet internally and with a gabled roof, and the hearth in one corner separated off by a low wall.

It is from the large earthwork enclosures of the

Windmill Hill folk, however, that we can recover more of their economic structure. These enclosures, roughly circular in plan, consist of one, or frequently two or three, concentric banks with wide intervals between, the material for the banks being provided by quarry-ditches roughly dug by gang labour and so interrupted by frequent causeways of undug soil. These causewayed camps crown low rounded hills in the undulating chalk country, as on Knap Hill in Wiltshire, Maiden Castle in Dorset, or Whitehawk near Brighton in Sussex, and when first identified as a type were interpreted as villages, since a considerable amount of occupational debris was found scattered in the silting of the ditches. But save in the exceptional instance of Hembury, in Devonshire, no trace of huts or houses has been found within the areas on excavation, and the hearths in the ditches can hardly be more than evidence of temporary occupation during reasonably warm weather. A reconsideration of the evidence leads to a more satisfactory explanation of their function.

An outstanding feature of the debris in the filling of the ditches is the large number of bones of young domestic animals—sheep, goat, pig, but especially ox —many showing the knife-cuts where sinews had been severed and the scratches from the hacking off of flesh. Furthermore, the ox-skulls when complete frequently showed systematic pole-axing—a hole over the left eye as if a sharp flint point had been driven in by a blow. These facts, coupled with an abundance of flint skin-scrapers, and tools of antler identical to those used by modern Eskimo tribes for preparing skins and furs, seem to point in one direction, to the annual reduction of herds at the end of the summer by killing off the young animals (a measure enforced by the scarcity of winter fodder in the absence of a root crop), and the utilization of their hides and sinews. The causewayed camps seem to be the seasonally occupied corrals of communities mainly engaged in stock-breeding, where the herds could be rounded up from a wide area of pasturage in the autumn, and the necessary slaughtering carried out. While the ancestral neolithic cultures of the Continent show evidence of a knowledge of spinning and weaving woollen fabric, there is no textile evidence from Britain, and skin clothing seems therefore likely to have been a by-product of these annual round-ups.

The cultivation of cereals is, however, indicated by finds of actual grain, probably wheat, and of impressions of grains of barley accidentally preserved in the rough domestic pottery: stone grain-rubbers also show that flour was ground during the camping period in the causewayed camps. But stock-breeding seems to have been the most important aspect of the neolithic farming economy of the Windmill Hill culture.

In some of the causewayed camps there is evidence of timber gateways and perhaps palisades—the frequent gaps in the ditches would give easy access when driving cattle in from outside, and temporary thorn fences might well have crowned the banks without leaving archæological evidence of their use. The distribution of the enclosures suggests that they served large areas of natural grazing on the chalk uplands that could not have been thickly wooded, though some sort of light forest and scrub must have existed, but one cannot discern the social system behind the recurrent rounding-up of herds. Communal ownership and collective effort in constructing and maintaining the enclosures might be urged, but on the other hand privately owned herds might graze mingled one with another, to be sorted out by ear-nicks or brand-marks at the annual gathering of the clans for stock-taking.

The question of woodland is of some importance. The botanical evidence suggests that the treeless grassy slopes of the downland so familiar to-day are an acquired and not a natural characteristic of the countryside of Wessex and Sussex, and that neolithic agriculture must have depended on some sort of forest clearance for its cultivation patches and its initial grazing grounds, however much these might be extended by the subsequent pasturing of increasingly large herds. We have seen how a flint axe of a sort was evolved by the mesolithic peoples of northern Europe in response to the new forest environment, and the dominance of the axe of chipped or ground flint or stone in the neolithic economy is equally apparent. The European evidence as a whole supports the thesis that extensive clearing of forests was begun by the first neolithic agriculturalists in all areas, sometimes accompanied by deliberate burning to destroy woodland, and in England (and the chalk areas of France and Belgium) we find interesting confirmation of the need for wood-cutters' axes. The best flint for flaking into tools is that obtained from subterranean horizontal seams that may run up to twenty feet beneath the surface of the Upper Chalk, and it is possible that superficial seams may have been encountered in digging the ditches of causewayed camps. However that may be, the essential geological facts of the occurrence of flint in chalk were known to the Windmill Hill folk, and the demand for a tree-felling tool, cheap and abundant, was met by the establishment of regular mining areas and factories designed for mass-production of flint axes.

The depth of these flint-mines, known from Wessex (e.g. Easton Down near Salisbury), Sussex (Cissbury and elsewhere), the Chilterns (Peppard), and East Anglia (Grimes Graves in Norfolk), was ultimately determined by the depth of the good horizontal flint seam from which the desired nodules could be prised. With a fairly shallow seam, it was more convenient to sink successive vertical shafts side by side, collecting flint from the small area exposed at the bottom of each, but with a twenty-foot deep seam, necessitating a huge vertical shaft with a diameter almost equal to its depth, it was found a saving of labour to drive lateral galleries horizontally to follow the seam for perhaps thirty or forty feet. Shaft after shaft was driven down to such a depth, until the underground galleries met and inter-locked in a strange underground network—as one mine was abandoned, the throw-out from a new pit would be tipped into it, filling the shaft but leaving the low galleries, along which a man can crawl, still open. The modern excavators found them with their roofs still smudged by the soot from smoky fat-lamps or torches, and with the miners' tools—'picks' or levers of red·deer antler, shovels of the shoulder-blades of oxen—still lying where they were abandoned, and even some-times retaining the imprint of the skin of the hand and the finger-prints in their chalky coating.

But these mine shafts and galleries, impressive though they are as sheer pieces of hard work in chalk-digging, were ancillary to the workshops in the open air above ground. Here the flint nodules were split and reduced to axes by an efficient system of economical flaking that yielded the required form with the minimum waste of effort, and which can be recognized as a standard technique on every site: the working debris sometimes shows how the various stages of the process were separately performed, presumably by different craftsmen, one roughing-out, another finishing, and so on. The eventual grinding and polishing of the axe, if carried out at all, was not undertaken at the factory sites, but perhaps by the individual who had acquired it by some form of barter or trade exchange—the existence of these large specialized workshops for tool production must imply trade of some kind. Polishing was worth while for added efficiency—a recent experiment showed that a seven-inch sapling could be cut down in five minutes with a polished stone axe, but took seven minutes with one of chipped flint only.

The aspects of the life of the Windmill Hill folk that we have been able to recover include, then, their essential economic background of stock-breeding and cattle-herding, with some cultivation of cereals, and an intimation of the seasonal rhythm of the agriculturists' year provided by the causewayed camps and their function in the reduction of the herds before winter. For cattle-grazing and for cultivation, cleared land was needed, and the axe factories and flint-mines show how the demand was met by a specialized industry. In the south-west, incidentally, stone axes of Cornish rocks were traded at least as far as southern Dorset. Of the village settlements that must surely have existed, we know nothing at present, but we must remember that causewayed camps as a class of neolithic enclosure were not recognized until about 1925. There remains another aspect to be considered, that of magical or religious beliefs, and of the ritual burial of the dead.

It must be confessed that there is evidence that scant respect was sometimes paid to the dead body by the Windmill Hill folk: dismembered fragments of human skeletons in telling proximity to animal bones in the hearths made in the sheltered ditches of the causewayed camps give more than a hint of cannibalism. But there are also deliberate graves of individuals on these sites and in isolation, sometimes it seems with a pot placed with the dead, perhaps containing food or drink. From the camps, too, come little phallic representations carved in chalk or bone, suggesting the mimetic magic of stock-breeders, and in one of the Grimes Graves flint-mines this magic was represented in still more vivid form. Here, a shaft had failed to strike flint, and perhaps the idea of the earth's abundance, so wished for, was embodied in the chalk figure of a fat and pregnant woman that had been set up on a ledge in a gallery, a carved chalk phallus below her and a heap of antler picks, symbolic of the miners' trade, piled about this curious little shrine.

But it is the burial rites that give us more information regarding neolithic beliefs about the otherworld. As we shall see later in this chapter, throughout the 'Western' neolithic culture provinces, from Spain to Brittany, and from the Pyrenees to the Orkneys, there was an underlying tradition of collective burial. A group of individuals united into some social or religious unit were buried together in a communal tomb, usually successively, as each individual died, though sometimes perhaps the bodies were temporarily reserved until a multiple funeral took place. In west and north Britain this collective burial tradition expressed itself in stone-built vaults or chambered tombs, which can be grouped into certain main classes of distinctive ground-plan, and which could normally be entered from time to time, as fresh burials were made. But the variant mode used by the Windmill Hill folk seems to have necessitated reservation of the bodies (presumably in all stages of decomposition) and their eventual collective burial under conditions that precluded further access to the tomb; or a long interval may have elapsed between the deposition of the first burial and the final closing of the tomb and completion of the covering mound.

The tombs in question are the conspicuous long mounds of earth known as the long barrows, piled up between two great quarry-ditches and conspicuous on the ridges of the chalk downs. Excavation has shown how the burials—which may range from a single individual to eighteen or twenty—are confined to a restricted space at one end of a mound that may be two or three hundred feet long, many of the skeletons (as might be expected if they had been brought to the site in a decayed state) being incomplete and disarticulated. Some barrows showed evidence of internal rectangular enclosures of turf revetting (Holdenhurst near Bournemouth), or of upright wooden stakes (Wor Barrow in Cranborne Chase, Dorset); in several, standing posts had been erected either near the burials or standing free of the barrow at one end (Thickthorn in Dorset, and Badshot near Farnham in Surrey for instance). Occasionally the skeletons had been burnt, partially and in a manner very different from the cremation later practised in the Bronze Age. Grave-goods deposited with the dead were few, flint arrow-heads or potsherds being among those found.

In the substance of the mound, and in the accumulated silting of the flanking quarry-ditches, were often abundant bones, and even articulated joints, of oxen and other domesticated beasts, suggesting funeral feasts, but of other ritual there is little trace except for enigmatic pits dug in the ground before the barrow was raised, perhaps connected with libations or food offerings.

But ritual of a most dramatic kind was implied by a very exceptional burial in an enormously long barrow at Maiden Castle in Dorset. This structure overlay the silted-up ditches of a causewayed camp and was no less than 1,790 feet long, and consisted of a mound 60 feet wide thrown up from parallel flanking ditches. At its eastern end, associated with 'ritual pits' of the type mentioned above and post-holes, was the burial of the body of a young adult man who had been deliberately hacked into joints on the spot—the head cut off first, the legs next, the arms last, and the pelvis split in two. The articulated limbs showed that the body was still flesh-covered when this ritual butchery took place: the head once removed, it had required three attempts to extract the brain from within the skull, the final and successful operation being to break through the occiput and base and so shatter the whole cranial vault.

These detailed and precise observations of archæologist and anatomist combine to reveal a gruesome piece of ritual—sacrifice and brain-eating, followed by the enormous labour of many men in digging and heaping the giant mound across the Dorset hill-top. With this in mind, we should not perhaps dismiss too lightly the claims of certain nineteenth-century archæologists that the condition of the skeletons they excavated from more normal long barrows in Wessex suggested human sacrifice in several instances.

On the Continent, true parallels to our Windmill Hill culture long barrows have not been identified, though somewhat similar tombs are known from Brittany —the archæology of the Channel coast of France eastward from here is little explored, and may still yield such burials and also causewayed camps, for earthworks dug in the same manner as these are certainly known on the eastern edge of the ' Western ' neolithic province in the Rhineland (though chronologically later than our English examples). At present we can only relate our Windmill Hill culture to those of neolithic France in general terms, with the reservation that Brittany seems an unlikely point of origin.

Within the area of primary settlement we can trace the consolidation of regional groups, characterized by distinctive pottery styles which begin to diverge from the simple forms common to both sides of the English Channel at the time of the initial colonization of southern England. In Sussex and, as we shall see, with the spread of the culture northwards, in East Anglia and farther north, similarities in pot forms with those in Belgium suggest developments influenced by a common mesolithic substratum in the population—an ancient unity established before the formation of the Channel and the southern part of the North Sea, but with individuality caused by this separation before the impact of neolithic cultures in the two areas.

Causewayed camps have been identified in the Thames Valley (near Abingdon) and on the chalk in Bedfordshire (near Dunstable), where the natural line of communication between Wessex and East Anglia still runs to-day as the Icknield Way. Botanical evidence suggests that at this time what is to-day the fenland was dry land with high-canopy forest, and by no means an impassable barrier between East Anglia and the chalk hills of Lincolnshire—along this route the Windmill Hill culture expanded and colonized, and on the Lincolnshire Wolds great long barrows as impressive as any in Wessex were built. In one that has been excavated (Giants' Hills, Skendleby) was found precisely the same reserved and collective burial as in Wiltshire or Dorset, with a massive timber-work enclosure around the edge of the mound which shows features that may indicate connexions with the Cotswolds or farther west.

North of the Humber another chalk area, that of the Yorkshire Wolds, was extensively colonized by the Windmill Hill culture, and the region seems to have become something of a backwater, developing local peculiarities in isolation after the main force of the neolithic move had gone on beyond. We shall follow this movement later, but for the present we may notice how in Yorkshire the long barrows cover not only inhumation burials, and collective burial may be found under round mounds as well (and this occurs as far south as near Royston in Herts, and perhaps in Wessex itself as an exceptional practice). But in Yorkshire we also see a development which may find its origin in the not infrequent partial cremation in Wessex long barrows already referred to, but taking the form of what seems to be the burning *in situ* of the bodies in a sort of flue built in the barrow—again, this may be long or round. There is much that is obscure in this distinctive Yorkshire manner of disposal of the dead in neolithic times, which spread as far as Northumberland (under a round mound) and, significantly as we shall see, to Westmorland (under a long cairn). The pottery from the Yorkshire tombs, and certain other objects (such as the peculiar skin-dressing combs identical with those already mentioned from the south English causewayed camps), relates the local neolithic to the Windmill Hill agriculturists, though domestic sites or the causewayed enclosures themselves have not yet been found.

A related form of the Yorkshire version of the Windmill Hill culture (attested at least by pottery) seems to have spread up into the Scottish lowlands (e.g. Bantaskine near Falkirk), and even to the Moray Firth (Easterton of Roseisle), but the finds are very scattered and the routes followed, by land or by sea, wholly unknown. But the Westmorland long cairn on Raisett Pike with cremation in the Yorkshire manner is more significant, and with this evidence of movement over towards the west coast of Britain we may take a remarkable site in Cumberland at Ehenside Tarn not far from St. Bees. Here the remains of a camp on a lake edge were recovered, with typical pots, corn-grinding stones, polished stone axes, some in their beechen hafts, and other wooden objects including three-pronged fish-spears, a curved throwing-stick, part of a bowl, and a canoe hollowed out from a tree trunk — all preserved in the wet peat and providing a welcome addition to our knowledge of the more perishable elements in the Windmill Hill culture.

A coastal settlement on the Solway Firth in Glenluce Bay has yielded neolithic pottery, again related to that of the far-off Yorkshire Wolds, and a grain impression on one sherd confirms the evidence of agriculture implied by the corn-grinding querns from the St. Bees site; but it is across the Irish Sea that we must look

for what appears to be the ultimate territory acquired
by the descendants of those Windmill Hill emigrants
from the Wessex homelands who made the trek towards
Lincolnshire and beyond. We shall find evidence later
on of the colonization of Ulster by seafarers whose
ancestors had known the sunny hill-slopes of Languedoc,
but it seems that when they arrived they did not find
northern Ireland inhabited solely by the descendants of
the mesolithic fisher-folk, whose simple culture we know
lingered long in that region side by side with the immigrant farmers and herdsmen. There is abundant evidence
of habitation sites belonging to people making pottery
of frankly Yorkshire type in Ulster—one at least is a very
large earthwork enclosure on Lyles Hill near Belfast.
The same folk mingled with the other neolithic colonists,
builders of collective tombs with stone-vaulted chambers
for successive burials, as is shown by a curious hybrid
tomb (Doey's Cairn, Dunloy) in which the plan is that
of chambered-tomb builders, but a cremation flue in the
Yorkshire manner is added rather incongruously. In this
tomb, as in others, fragments of Yorkshire-derived pottery
have been found, distinguishable from the intrusive wares
of south French derivation. We shall see later on that
there is reason to think that the sequence of arrival of
neolithic colonists in Ulster was one in which the move
from over the Irish Sea (perhaps from Cumberland or
from Galloway, or from both regions) was earlier than
that of the arrival of the builders of the stone-built
chambered tombs, but the two groups must have merged
sufficiently for both to be entitled indifferently to burial
in such funeral vaults.

In Ulster the pottery traditions at least of Yorkshire
or of Lyles Hill seem to have lasted very long: like

Yorkshire itself, it became a backwater after the initial colonization. The Isle of Man was also included in the region where such pots were in use, but they may be late arrivals there, though there is some not very decisive evidence of a cremation flue in a cairn on that island.

We must now turn to the neolithic cultures which reached Britain by the western sea-ways, and effected colonization of those coastal areas which are to-day Cornwall, Wales, and western and northern Scotland, with the Isles, as well as (it seems) the greater part of Ireland. The evidence on which our knowledge of these colonizing movements is based is very one-sided, consisting almost entirely of tombs, with very rare settlement sites: however, grave-goods, especially the pots, deposited with the dead in these tombs, give us in some areas at least an added cultural dimension to that provided by the type and plan of the funeral vaults, which for the most part are our only clues in sorting out the regional divergences in a closely linked series of cultures. The fact that the movements were seaborne results in an often very discontinuous distribution pattern, but some of the main lines now seem reasonably clear.

Earlier in this chapter, when dealing with the long barrows of the Windmill Hill culture, we noticed the tradition of collective burial, so widely spread through the Western neolithic cultures of Europe. In the Mediterranean, communal vaults hewn out of the limestone rock are a tomb-type going back well into the early third millennium and beyond, and in southern France and again in Spain we find not only rock-cut chambers of this type, but stone versions built above ground, either as a corbelled vault, or by massive stone uprights and cap-stones in a true 'megalithic' manner, but in either case covered by a cairn. There seems to have been an early, perhaps primary, division of tomb-type into two—one in which a more or less circular burial chamber is approached by a well-defined passage, the whole under a round cairn ('passage-graves'); the other having an elongated, parallel-sided chamber or gallery with no functional distinction of a passage, and usually under a long cairn ('gallery-graves'). Of these ground-plans, which in their typologically later stages often become confusingly similar, the passage-grave form seems to have been that carried by seaborne colonization round the Atlantic coasts from south Spain to Portugal, and thence to Brittany, where the second strain is also present, apparently as the result of a landward movement from the region of the Gulf of Lions and the Pyrenees. In Britain, both strains are present, and can sometimes be clearly distinguished, occupying mutually exclusive areas of colonization, but it must be urged again that a hard and fast classification of every megalithic tomb into one or other group is neither possible nor likely to bear much relation to the actual course of events in neolithic times.

The divergences in ground-plan clearly embody some important distinction in ritual and belief, though with a fundamental unity, in the same sense that a Nonconformist chapel differs from a Roman Catholic church, and both from one of the Greek Orthodox rite. It seems likely that the megalithic chambered tombs were each a focus of ritual to a degree unshared by a simple burial in an earth-dug grave, and we shall indeed see archæological evidence of rites involving ceremonial fires, libations, and sacrifice before the entrance of some of these monuments; and for the proper observance of a primitive liturgy certain sanctified details of architecture would have to be perpetuated, whether in the Pyrenees or in the Hebrides. But we must remember that in classifying these tombs we may be doing no more than defining the boundaries of religious sects, and that in this classification we must be on our guard against confusing poverty, or an unsuitable building material, with heterodoxy. The tin tabernacle may be no less orthodox than the medieval parish church.

With these preliminaries, we can conveniently turn to the various regions colonized by the makers of these tombs. A distinctive regional variant is represented by a number of monuments mainly in South Wales and Gloucestershire, defined as the Severn-Cotswold group. Here pure typology appears to break down—elements of both passage-grave and gallery-grave traditions seem present (the long cairns covering the chambers are particularly suggestive of the latter; some chamber plans perhaps less so), but fortunately a very comparable group of tombs, which seem good claimants for ancestry, can be identified in west France, round the mouth of the Loire and up to southern Brittany. The Severn-Cotswold tombs therefore suggest a restricted immigration from that region, up the Bristol Channel, and making its first landings in Gower and at the foot of Mendip and the Cotswold Hills.

The main areas of colonization were the Brecknock-shire Black Mountains (e.g. the cairn at Ty Isaf, Talgarth), the limestone areas of Cotswold (many tombs including Belas Knap and Hetty Pegler's Tump), and a rather individual region in north Wiltshire, around Avebury, and Somerset (e.g. Stony Littleton, Wellow)

—perhaps a separate intrusion along the Mendips. The typologically early tombs, nearest to the Breton examples, have a plan with one or more pairs of transepts opening from the main chamber; the entrance is recessed within a double sweep of stone walling demarcating a forecourt area, and this walling is carried round the edges of the trapeze-shaped cairn. Such tombs have been excavated at Notgrove and Nympsfield in the Cotswolds. A progressive degeneration of plan can be traced, in which the entrance loses its functional significance and becomes a purely ritual feature.

In the chambers the skeletons showed evidence of successive burials, the earlier burials being swept aside or stacked away to the rear of the vault as new corpses were deposited on the floor—in one instance, at least (Lanhill near Chippenham), the long bones were ranged along the back of the chamber, the six or seven skulls along the two sides. It is clear that after each funeral the forecourt area was filled with earth and stones so that the entrance was completely masked: the elaborate dry walling round the cairn was never exposed at all, but was purely a ritual feature. In the forecourt were remains of hearths, and of shattered pots suggesting ritual breaking after a libation, and occasional potsherds or flint arrow-heads accompanied the dead, though there seems to have been no regular deposit of grave-goods.

These Severn-Cotswold tombs seem to run parallel in time with the neighbouring Windmill Hill culture: the final forecourt blocking of more than one tomb contains pottery of types which appear in Wessex at the time of the submergence of the Windmill Hill culture there, late in the neolithic, but one great chambered cairn, at West Kennet in north Wiltshire, continued in use until the beginning of the Bronze Age in that region.

A very important area of colonization, and one whose continental antecedents seem reasonably clear, lies at the head of the Irish Sea, and since its main ports of entry appear to have been in the Clyde estuary and round Carlingford Lough in northern Ireland, it has been named the Clyde-Carlingford culture. Over a large area —which includes the southern islands of the Hebrides, Arran, Bute, and Kintyre, as well as Galloway in Scotland, extends southwards to include the Isle of Man and touch Anglesey, and comprises most of Ulster, with outlying colonies as far as Sligo and County Mayo in Ireland—evidence of this culture can be traced, largely by the characteristic tomb-plans, but also accompanied by a distinctive pottery style.

The tombs have, typically, an elongated burial gallery divided into segments by high sill-slabs or by side jamb-stones: in Scotland frequently and in Ireland invariably this gallery opens on to a forecourt demarcated by a crescentic setting of uprights joined by panels of dry-walling, and the whole is set at one end of a long cairn, often trapeze-shaped in the manner of the Severn-Cotswold tombs. There are many sub-varieties — in Ireland a series of progressive degenerations can be traced as one goes westwards—and it is not certain that the elaborate monuments with crescentic façades are the earliest in Scotland. But generically the ancestors of these Clyde-Carlingford tombs belong to the gallery-grave group of south France and the western Mediterranean—the crescentic façade is a conspicuous feature in the chambered tombs of Sardinia, has relatives in Malta, and may have prototypes in rock-cut tombs in

Sicily; and the simple gallery-grave of south France, normally in a long cairn, is segmented in the Scottish manner in the Pyrenees and in Apulia (another area of secondary colonization from the Gulf of Lions). The decorated pottery recovered from many of the tombs in the Clyde-Carlingford culture has very close parallels in a class of neolithic wares in south France, where it follows on the earliest fabric, ancestral to that of Windmill Hill. It is therefore to a region comprising south France and the Pyrenees that we may look for an origin for our neolithic colonization of the head of the Irish Sea—curiously enough, to much the same region as that from which the first mesolithic fisher-folk of Oronsay seem to have come.

The tombs of the Clyde-Carlingford folk are so sited as to suggest the family vaults of small communities settling on the patches of good farming land: a settlement in Bute, probably of the local tomb-builders, has produced grains of wheat as well as corn-grinding stones, and the bones of domesticated ox, pig, sheep, and goat were found as the remnants of funeral offerings in many tombs. Stone axes imply some tree-felling, and there is evidence of a local trade in pitchstone and perhaps flint, while in the Hebrides a primitive potters' workshop and kilns were found, though there is no evidence that the wares were exported beyond the island on which they were made. The broken pottery and fires in the forecourts of the tombs imply ritual in the same manner as the Cotswold people.

We have already seen that a branch of the Windmill Hill culture arrived in Ulster approximately contemporaneously with the Clyde-Carlingford colonization of the head of the Irish Sea. But the fact that none of the very recognizable Windmill Hill pottery (of the type of that from Lyles Hill in Ulster for instance) has been found in the Clyde-Carlingford tombs in Scotland, though it is abundant in Ireland, suggests that the Scottish colonization was the earlier event. The Windmill Hill tribes, ultimately of Yorkshire origin, on coming to the west coast seem to have found the regions northwards already in the hands of neolithic colonists, whereas Ulster was still available for settlement, with a small population of mesolithic fisher-folk. The Irish branch of the Clyde-Carlingford culture might be the result of a fresh move from Europe, or (more probably) a secondary colonization from Scotland.

From the regions of primary settlement, traces of the culture can be found in tombs of related types in southern Ireland (Ballynamona, County Waterford), west Wales (Pentre Ifan, Pembrokeshire), Cornwall, and even Dorset (The Grey Mare, Portisham). The relative dating of the first colonies in Scotland or Ireland seems, on various grounds, to be quite possibly as early as the first establishment of the Windmill Hill culture in southern England, though many of the Irish tombs at least must be later, for, as we have seen, contact with the derivative Windmill Hill culture of Yorkshire origin seems decisive on this point. The use of the tombs (as with all such monuments) of course persisted in outlying regions for many centuries, up to (and in Ireland beyond) the local arrival of metal-using people with single-grave traditions of burial in the first half of the second millennium.

In Ireland there are other large groups of chambered tombs coming formally within the gallery-grave tradition on the criteria of their plans, but little is known of their precise archæological context, while the same may be said for the large number of so-called ' dolmens ' here and in Wales and Cornwall. Many of these seem poor relations or degenerations of gallery-graves or passage-graves indifferently: now so frequently free-standing monuments, they must originally, like the other chambered tombs, have been covered by a cairn or barrow.

The most remarkable and best known of the Irish chambered tombs, however, belong very clearly to the passage-grave tradition, and this can be traced as a colonizing movement making its first decisive landfall well south of the Clyde-Carlingford region, in the neighbourhood of Dublin. The type is consistently the chamber with approach passage beneath a circular cairn, and contrary to the practice of, for instance, the Clyde - Carlingford or Severn - Cotswold folk, these tombs are frequently grouped in cemeteries on hill-tops. From one of the most notable cemeteries, that near the Boyne containing the famous New Grange tomb, these passage-graves have been classed as the Boyne culture, and it can be seen to have spread north-westwards across Ireland by way of Loughcrew and Carrowkeel to Sligo Bay, and also northwards (e.g. Cross, County Antrim), while scattered sites extend as far south as County Limerick.

Some of the Boyne culture tombs (such as Tibradden, County Dublin) have a chamber built of corbelled vaulting; others again have this technique combined with upright walling slabs (as at New Grange), or the construction is wholly of massive flat stones (Carrowmore, County Sligo), but the essential features are nevertheless preserved throughout. In these tombs the forecourt ritual, so important in the groups we have already discussed, seems minimized or absent, and attention is concentrated on the features of passage and chamber. This, in its most striking aspect, takes the form of elaborate ornament incised or ' pecked ' on the flat surfaces of the stones, in zigzags, concentric circles, spirals, lozenges, and other geometric forms, many, however, recognizable as stylized representations of a pair of eyes or a human face. Such patterning needs upright stones for its reception, and cannot be executed on a corbelled vault; at New Grange, indeed, the upright stones of passage and chamber, so many of which are decorated, have no structural function, but stand in front of a dry-stone wall that carries the cap-stones of the corbelled vault. As one goes westwards, this decoration ceases (though it may have been carried out in now-vanished paint), and the most westerly passage - grave cemetery, near Sligo, shows degeneration in building technique as well.

Within the lateral chambers in many tombs stood huge shallow stone bowls similar to those found in the passage-graves of Iberia, which very closely resemble many of the Boyne series; and here, too, is painted ornament at least, but the incised and pecked Boyne techniques are best represented in Breton tombs. It is then to Iberia and Brittany that we must look for the origins of the Boyne culture, for there all the classic features of passage and chamber within the round cairn, often with a conspicuous bounding circle of large stones, can be found.

The material culture of the Boyne folk, as implied by the grave-goods in the tombs, seems curiously insular, but a few Iberian or Breton contacts are perceptible. The bodies seem to have been partially cremated, and the bones gathered into bags fastened by huge bone pins, some of types known in Early Bronze Age Portugal;

there are distinctive little stone pendants like miniature mace-heads and others of Iberian forms. The pottery is a very coarse fabric with roughly stabbed and impressed ornament which has some vague affinities with neolithic wares in north-west Scotland. Agriculture is attested by grains of wheat from beneath the cairn of one tomb, but settlement sites are not definitely known, though a large group of circular stone-built hut foundations near the Carrowkeel cemetery might be contemporary with the tombs. The chronological position of the Boyne culture is difficult to assess. Recent evidence suggests that in Iberia many passage-graves may not be so early as formerly assumed. There is a growing tendency among archæologists to regard the passage-graves of the British Isles as little, if at all, earlier than the first use of metal in these islands. The tomb-types are early in the Atlantic coast sequence, but some of the Irish grave-goods (such as the pendants and pottery 'food-vessels', which need not always be secondary) have their best parallels in Bronze Age England.

Near Limerick, at Lough Gur, and in the Isle of Man, at Ronaldsway, large rectangular houses divided into aisles by two rows of internal posts have been found, in the former site with others of circular plan. At both sites there is clear evidence of neolithic date, but the pottery in the Irish site does not relate to any types known from the chambered tombs, while in the Isle of Man the culture has interesting affinities to that of Skara Brae described later in this chapter. The relationship of these very interesting settlement sites with the various chambered-tomb provinces is therefore still obscure. In the Isle of Man cremation-cemeteries of the same culture as that of the Ronaldsway house are known.

A small group of closely interrelated chambered tombs is known in the Scilly Islands and the Land's End district, and across the Irish Sea in the neighbourhood of Tramore. These tombs have small circular cairns, and the elongated burial chamber seems a likely development from passage-grave types: the grave-goods from Scilly at least suggest a rather late date at the end of the local neolithic, while from one of the tombs and from a midden with occupational debris come saddle-quern fragments indicating corn-grinding. The chambered tombs cluster so thickly there as to suggest that these were sacred islands of the west, dim traditions of which found their way to the classical writers centuries later.

The distribution-pattern of neolithic tomb-types in western Scotland shows that in the territory of the Clyde-Carlingford people passage-graves hardly exist, but northwards in the Hebrides, Caithness, Sutherland, and the Orkney and Shetland Islands, various forms of passage-grave are the exclusive type. This suggests that the Clyde-Carlingford folk were already in occupation when offshoots of the Boyne and allied cultures were seeking territory northwards by sea-routes which might either have started from Sligo Bay or from Antrim, but which did not touch suitably unoccupied lands until the Firth of Lorne was reached. This may support the view that there was some interval of time between the two events. From the Firth of Lorne, the Great Glen offers a natural highway across Scotland to the shores of the Moray Firth, and in the Inverness and Nairn district a group of passage-graves—the Clava group—show typologically early features such as the circular corbelled chamber. These tombs might represent an early move of passage-grave people from Ireland, probably by the Antrim route, but archæological confirmation of the typology is not available in the absence of modern excavation of the tombs.

In Skye and in North Uist, however, such excavation has shown that passage-graves such as Clettraval and Unival were being built as early as some of those of the Clyde-Carlingford group, well before the local advent of the Early Bronze Age, and the tomb plans here are within the limit of variations of the normal passage-grave tradition (though in one instance perhaps showing interaction with Clyde-Carlingford ideas of planning). The distribution of the Hebridean tombs suggests the use of a sea-route leading to the west coasts of the islands, where there are better agricultural land and natural harbours than on the east. When we reach Caithness we begin to find that the classic tradition is being developed along very individual lines—long cairns and crescentic façades as at Yarrow and Camster look like gallery-grave features, unless they are a resurgent element always present in the chambered-tomb tradition as a whole. But the culture is not impoverished, if magnitude of construction is any criterion, for huge cairns covering chambers with fine corbelled vaults continued to be built, as if the religious tradition were finding a secret strength in this remote and isolated community.

This individualism and undiminished vigour in monumental tomb construction seems to burst into a fierce blaze of fanaticism in the remarkable chambered tombs of Orkney. Here every eccentricity of architecture appears —two-storey tombs (Taiversoe Tuack for example), the cap-stones of one chamber forming the floor of another, and two separate passages from opposite sides of the cairn; fantastically high vaulting carried up fourteen feet above the narrow chamber floor; more than one tomb-type is entirely peculiar to the Islands. The famous tomb of Maes Howe is as orthodox as New Grange, and in most of the abnormalities the underlying elements that have been exaggerated or diminished can be traced back to more normal prototypes; but there is one class of tomb, the so-called ' Stalled Cairns ', known especially on Rousay, which may have an individual origin, at least in part. In these the chamber is an elongated oblong filling most of the available space in a very well built rectangular cairn with revetment walls, and divided by lateral stone slabs projecting from both sides to form compartments or ' stalls ', in which the corpses were laid on stone-built benches. While similarly placed stones are a constructional feature in more orthodox passage-graves both in Orkney and in Caithness, the arrangement in the stalled cairns does strongly suggest a stone version of the neolithic long houses with two rows of posts which we have noted in Ireland and the Isle of Man, the corpses in the tombs lying much where the beds would naturally be placed in the house of the living.

As in the Clyde-Carlingford province, it is possible to see that the stalled cairns of Orkney at least were placed in relation to the available arable land. In the island of Rousay, which has been closely studied and in which numerous excavations have been carried out, fourteen such tombs exist, all likely to be more or less contemporary, and all occupying positions corresponding to the modern concentrations of crofts in the twelve square miles of potential or actual arable land that the island contains. In the eighteenth century this farming land supported a population of nearly 800 persons, but a substantial reduction of this figure would obviously be necessary in any estimate of a neolithic population with more primitive agriculture. There is evidence from the cairns of the autumnal killing of young cattle, just as in the Windmill Hill culture, and the larder was augmented by hunting red deer, and by fishing for wrasse, bream, conger, and other fish.

The material culture known from the tombs includes a distinctive type of pottery of which a related form is known from the Hebrides, and there is evidence of the use of the tombs in late neolithic and Early Bronze Age times—though what this may mean in terms of actual chronology in such a remote region is another matter. In the Shetlands is another regional variant of the passage-grave type of tomb peculiar to those islands, but here there has been no excavation to help us in defining its cultural connexions.

This survey of the main areas of neolithic habitation in Britain characterized by the use of stone-built chambered tombs for collective burial has been of necessity sketchy and incomplete, but it serves to indicate the basic distribution-pattern as we know it. There remains one curiously isolated group of such tombs to be mentioned, in the Medway valley in Kent. To understand the Medway tombs we must consider the further voyages of the folk who built chambered tombs, beyond the Atlantic coasts and beyond Britain.

By a route which may have been through the Pentland Firth or perhaps more probably may have been up the English Channel, more than one group of neolithic colonists reached Scandinavia and North Germany, there to introduce the arts of agriculture and stock-breeding to the mesolithic inhabitants. These immigrants practised collective burial in chambered tombs, and in the broadest sense belong to the same group of Atlantic coast cultures within the Western neolithic group as those who settled ·in western and northern Britain. But their tombs took on a distinctive regional character in their new home, and in the Medway tombs at Coldrum, Kits Coty, or Addington we can recognize a secondary colonization westwards, probably from the regions now Holland and North Germany rather than from Scandinavia, perhaps not unconnected with other late neolithic folk movements from the same region and the coming of the first metal-using peoples to east England.

We can see therefore that the contribution of the Western neolithic cultures to Britain was very great: the settlement of the Windmill Hill folk in south England, and of the related peoples denoted by the various forms of collective chambered tombs in the west and north, meant the introduction of the basic agricultural economy which lies behind the whole subsequent course of British prehistory and history. Chronologically, this settlement seems to have taken place in the centuries immediately after 2500 B.C.: it can never have been a simple process, but inevitably an interlocking series of moves of tribes, clans, and families by boat or overland, settling and farming for a generation or so, and then perhaps moving on, so that their territory would be taken over by newcomers. At the social organization behind these groups we can only guess, but the large patriarchal ' undivided family ' or clan seems a likely enough unit, though the status of those who were entitled to burial within the great hill-top tombs of Loughcrew or Carrowkeel may not have been that of the crofter families of Arran or Rousay — here is more than a suspicion of kingship.

Physically, the allied groups within the Western neolithic culture seem very homogeneous, small, slender in build, long-headed and often with strong noses of an almost aquiline profile. In Wiltshire, Lincolnshire, and in Kent, the skulls from collective tombs show strong family likenesses within the group entitled to burial in the chamber: the bodies of the aged were often bowed and locked in rheumatoid arthritis, their teeth worn down with the grit contained in flour ground on primitive grinding stones. The colour of their hair and eyes is wholly unknown, and one must remember that skulls of indistinguishable form within the dolichocephalic group may come from fair or dark individuals.

In addition to the neolithic cultures within the Western group, there is in Britain evidence for a substantial contribution, within the second half of the third millennium B.C., from cultures lying within the Nordic group centred on Scandinavia, to which reference has been made already. We have seen that in mesolithic times eastern England lay on the fringe of the Maglemose culture-province, at a time when land communications were still possible across what is now the southern part of the North Sea; and though land subsidence submerged this area and brought about the formation of the English Channel in late Boreal times, yet links still seem to have remained between the Baltic and East Anglia well into the third millennium. In the Baltic countries, from Finland to Denmark, there had grown up a network of related cultures, based on a mixture of Maglemose hunter-fisher survivals and of intrusive elements, including the craft of the potter and probably some rudimentary agriculture, whose origins lie in the steppe lands. Their pottery is coarse and heavy and, in complete contradistinction to the smooth leathery wares of the Western neolithic, is normally elaborately ornamented with patterns made by impressing various forms of twisted cords, blunt-toothed combs, the articulating ends of small animal or bird bones, or various forms of tools to make pits in the surface—the whole effect being a rudimentary pottery style imitating basketry prototypes.

In Britain pottery ornamented in precisely these distinctive styles is known from many sites in southern and eastern England, and from scattered finds elsewhere, and the culture it represents has been named from an important habitation site near Peterborough. Such a marked similarity with the Scandinavian material must imply continued contacts maintained across the North Sea, but the British pottery has its own distinct individuality, owing, as we shall see, to local contacts with other neolithic groups. But the important feature of the Peterborough and its allied cultures, so far as we can distinguish them at present, is their very strong mesolithic element. The distribution of settlements is along the rivers and on the sea-coasts; evidence of agriculture is scanty; flint types include arrow-heads and other implements of distinctively mesolithic derivation. Naturalistic engravings of animals in a manner ultimately of mesolithic origin seem also attributable to Peterborough folk. We shall see evidence of mobility and of long cross-country trade connexions that suggests the trails known to hunting bands rather than the more sedentary life of the farmer, and in general we have to complete our picture of neolithic Britain by setting over against the agricultural communities, relatively static, cultivating and grazing on the easily cleared soils, the descendants of the mesolithic hunter-fisher folk, who, having acquired some of the neolithic arts, still continued to live according to a more ancient mode by river, marsh, or seashore.

Such cultural borrowing must have taken place independently in many areas where the intrusive agriculturalists came into contact with the aboriginal inhabitants. In northern Ireland, for instance, there is a primitive culture which seems to have been centred on catching and smoking fish by the banks of the river Bann, which looks very like mesolithic folk picking up pottery-making, at least, from the neolithic colonists of the region. Elsewhere in Britain we can distinguish two main groups on the grounds of pottery styles and other features of their material culture.

The Peterborough culture already referred to is known from village sites, with hut-foundations scooped below the surface of the ground, and in the Thames Valley and East Anglia the pottery shapes seem to have been modified by influence from the contemporary local Windmill Hill styles. In Sussex what looks like an early phase of Peterborough pottery appears during the period of occupation of the causewayed camp of Whitehawk near Brighton, but in Wessex the arrival of its makers seems to mark the end of the local Windmill Hill culture there—a camp site at Avebury in north Wiltshire has carefully built circular hearths, but no recognizable trace of houses. Here, and in East Anglia, it is clear that the Peterborough folk were much concerned with flint-mining and axe-making, side by side with the Windmill Hill people, and at Grimes Graves in Norfolk two little engravings of deer, in a naturalistic manner ultimately Upper Palæolithic in tradition, compare well with similar survivals of such an art-style in Scandinavia among the descendants of the mesolithic inhabitants. Further scattered finds of Peterborough pottery extend the range of the culture to Wales, Northumberland, and southern Scotland, but the implications of these sites will be considered later.

The second culture which seems to have its roots in the northern European mesolithic is that which may be called the Skara Brae culture, from a site in Orkney. The distinguishing feature by which this culture was first identified is a peculiar pottery, not ornamented with cord-impressed patterns, in contradistinction to Peterborough ware, but with a system of shallow grooving and pitting on the one hand, and of raised plastic ornament on the other. The antecedents of this ware outside Britain are not clear, but there is a widespread late-neolithic European tradition of plastic ornament which shows itself in regions as far distant as Spain and Holland, and it is to the more northerly regions that we should relate the Skara Brae material.

While the culture is most abundantly represented in the Orkney sites to be described below, it is nevertheless known from many southern English sites from the Wash to Wessex, notably at Clacton-on-Sea and at Woodhenge in Wiltshire. The very explicit pottery parallels make the relationship with Orkney undoubted, if puzzling, but the peculiar conditions of the northern sites render generalizations from them very dangerous if applied to, for instance, Wessex. None of the south

English habitation sites with grooved ware has produced
evidence of the houses or village lay-out, and its most
interesting associations seem to be with a class of ritual
monument best known in the succeeding Bronze Age.
This will be referred to again below in more detail
when we come to deal with the religious aspects of the
Peterborough and Skara Brae cultures, but for the
present we may profitably turn to the wealth of evidence
for the daily life and material culture of the Orkney
communities.

At the two village sites of Skara Brae and Rinyo in
Orkney, the makers of the characteristic pottery already
described lived in single-roomed stone-built huts or
houses of roughly sub-rectangular ground-plan, about
15 feet square internally, and built together into a closely
knit complex with narrow alleys between. The roofs
were probably of turf and sods on some form of rafters,
more likely to be bones from stranded whales than wood,
which is thought to have been rare in the islands. This
apparent lack of timber led to the internal fittings of
the huts, for which in normal circumstances wood would
be used, being made of the easily split local flagstone,
and so we have a peculiarly detailed knowledge of these
features. A central square hearth, on which peat was
burnt, was, at Rinyo at least, often flanked by a small
clay oven; in the floor were sunk one or two square
' boxes ' lined with slabs, in which it is thought that
limpets and other shell-fish could be kept alive in water.
To the right and left of the door were the beds against
the wall, formed by upright slabs and stone ' bed-
posts ', filled with bracken or heather when in use, and
it is noticeable that the right-hand bed is the larger, and
presumably that of the master of the house. Against the

wall opposite the door was a dresser, made of two shelves supported and separated by other stone slabs, and in the thickness of the wall by the beds were small cup-boards or 'keeping-places'.

Within the dark interiors of these huts, the air thick with acrid peat-smoke, there seems to have been, at the time of their use, a state of indescribable filth and disorder. The floors are found stained with sewage and strewn with bones and shells discarded from successive meals; in the beds there fell down among the loose bed-ding not only personal possessions such as bone pins or beads, but oddments such as a calf's skull or a shoulder-blade shovel. Such debris as could not be tolerated in the huts even under these conditions was taken outside and piled over the complex of buildings, so that in its later days the village was practically subterranean beneath its own midden.

There is evidence of extensive cattle-breeding (in-cluding gelding to produce a proportion of bullocks in the herds), but none of any form of grain-growing. Limpets and other shell-fish were largely eaten, and occasional deer and sea-fowl killed, but curiously enough there is hardly any evidence of fishing or seal-hunting. No textiles or their means of production can be traced, and clothing must have been made from skins. Various forms of bone pin were made, as well as beads, and hard stones were laboriously ground into elaborate decorative spiked shapes.

These curious communities were entirely self-support-ing, with a strictly neolithic economy, but in terms of actual chronology are likely to have survived many centuries after the establishment of metal-using cultures elsewhere in Britain. But in Orkney itself they antedate the local arrival of the people associated with the earliest use of bronze, though the appearance of these folk in such a remote spot may be centuries later than their advent in south England about 1800 B.C. In southern and eastern England, however, sites producing pottery of the Skara Brae type, while they seem to belong to the end of the neolithic period, again are earlier than the coming of the earliest Beaker folk and the dawn of the Bronze Age, even in this region of primary settlement.

We have already seen that the Peterborough people were concerned in the flint-axe industry and in mining, but they seem also to have played an important part in the organization of a related piece of primitive mercantile activity which was to have repercussions in the Bronze Age. Already in earlier neolithic times Windmill Hill folk in Dorset were importing from Cornwall axes made of tough greenstones almost certainly from Cornwall, but in general the chalk country was self-sufficient with its local flint manufacture. With the appearance of Peterborough folk in Wessex, however, we find increasing numbers of these axes of geologically foreign stones in use, and petrological examination is beginning to sort out the regions from which they were derived—Cornwall, North Wales, and the Lake District appear to be among the most important areas with which Wessex and the Thames Valley traded in the late neolithic period.

Near Penmaenmawr in North Wales an actual axe factory has been identified, where outcrops of a suitable rock occur and where workshop debris still strews the mountain-side. The rock flakes well, and the technique of manufacture closely recalls that of the factory sites near the flint-mines. Characteristic pottery shows the presence of Peterborough folk in the region, and axes of Penmaenmawr stone have been traced southwards to Wessex and eastwards to the Fens. Another factory site has been recognized on Langdale Pike in the Lake District, again trading its products southwards to the Thames Valley and beyond.

A close connexion of the Peterborough people with this long-distance trade seems likely not only from the evidence of associated finds, but also from the inherent probabilities of the situation. The old hunter-fisher folk, faced with the coming of an intrusive agricultural economy, had partly adopted elements from this and partly set about establishing themselves in an advantageous position within the new framework of society as it was dimly forming. They knew the river routes and the hunters' trails through the forests and across the moorlands: perhaps it was their skill as hunters that made them welcome at the flint-mines as suppliers of the constantly needed red deer antlers for levering out the chalk blocks. Already by birth and origin outside the clan or tribal systems of the Western neolithic folk, they could move freely as traders from one region to another, vagrant gipsies among the settled farming communities, middlemen in the trade in stone axes or anything they could turn to their advantage (good basketry may have been a profitable side-line). It is by such folk, surely, that these long routes from Wiltshire to North Wales, or from Langdale Pike to the Middle Thames, were first traversed—the dispossessed hunters, unwilling to settle down to the slow routine of the farm, who by their wanderings joined the rich agricultural lands of southern England to those regions far to the west and north whence succeeding generations in Wessex were to obtain the metal ores their own land could not supply. The trade in foreign stone axes linked the purchasing power to the potential natural supply, and laid the foundation of the brilliant Wessex Bronze Age.

We know as yet little of the burials and ritual aspects of the Peterborough and allied folk, but what little we do know is intriguing. Makers of Peterborough pots were apparently entitled to burial in neolithic chambered tombs in the Cotswolds and elsewhere, and in Derbyshire and again in North Wales stone-built tombs against the rock in cave shelters contained burials of the same culture. But in the Thames Valley at Stanton Harcourt, and in Bedfordshire at Dunstable, are burials of single skeletons within circular ditches, and in one instance under a round barrow, which seem almost certainly of the Peterborough culture, and one of these is definitely earlier than an Early Bronze Age burial. Single-grave burial is typical of the Early Bronze Age in Britain as abroad, but may have earlier antecedents, and with these burials we may take certain large circular monuments which seem to be open sanctuaries, with a bank and ditch enclosing an area in which timber uprights sometimes have stood. As a class these have been attributed in the past to an Early Bronze Age innovation, but evidence in Wiltshire and the Thames Valley suggests that they may also be referred to the grooved-ware group at least of the late neolithic population, before the arrival of the Beaker immigrants. Burials by cremation occur in these monuments, and in the local Manx culture of grooved-ware affinities already referred to in connexion with its rectangular houses.

The chronological position of the Peterborough and Skara Brae cultures seems to be such that while they may both in their origins go back as early as the settlement phase of the Windmill Hill culture (and perhaps antedate it, though with what degree of agricultural economy they may then be credited is uncertain), they certainly survive longer in southern England at all events. The natural stratigraphy of the Fenland peats has provided us with a climatic and botanical horizon for the Windmill Hill culture in that region, and an axe which is an undoubted product of the Penmaenmawr axe factory is in the same peats stratified significantly higher, though still earlier than the Early Bronze Age. On the foreshore in certain parts of Essex round Clacton there is an old land-surface which is now covered by a clay layer and is below present high-water mark: the submergence implied here is echoed in semi-marine clay deposits overlying peat in the Fens and both may be equated with a date round about 1900 B.C. In both Windmill Hill ware lies beneath the clay, but on the Essex coast there occurs also Skara Brae pottery and the earliest Bronze Age beakers. In Wessex, Peterborough occupation appears in more or less deserted causewayed camps, though one site can be shown to be pre-Beaker, and in Anglesey there appears to be a Peterborough settlement (significantly containing axes of Penmaenmawr stone) antedating a chambered tomb of typologically degenerate form. In Orkney, as we have seen, a scaling-down in chronology is probably necessary, though the relationship of Skara Brae pottery to Early Bronze Age beakers is relatively the same as in the south.

As we shall see in the next chapter, the British Bronze Age seems to be based, in large part, on cultural traditions bound up with the Peterborough complex of cultures rather than those of the Western neolithic groups. In the pottery styles this debt is obvious—much British Early and all Middle Bronze Age pottery follows insular traditions of cord-ornament and other features closely linked with Peterborough styles but unknown on the Continent—and we have seen that the late neolithic trade in stone axes may well anticipate the subsequent routes of metal-merchants. The universal adoption of cremation in Middle Bronze Age times may be related to the late neolithic practice already mentioned. But the communities in the Western neolithic tradition seem to have contributed little, save the basic and essential fact of the agricultural pattern of existence, even in the regions of the west and north where they were so long established and which were reached comparatively late by the new immigrant groups from the European mainland who landed in the south-east lowlands. Even the farming tradition may have waned during the Bronze Age and been partially replaced by increased pastoralism and hunting, harking back to Peterborough and even mesolithic origins.

CHAPTER IV

THE BRONZE AGE

THE world of neolithic Britain was, as we have seen, one of agricultural communities, perhaps more of pastoralists than of intensive growers of corn, all ultimately based on the Western neolithic tradition of continental Europe. Side by side with these there existed other rather less clearly defined groups of peoples, all probably agriculturalists or pastoralists, whose origins went back to the ancient Forest cultures of the Baltic and the corded-ware traditions of the steppe countries. Flint and stone were exclusively used for cutting tools, and in the provision of an adequate supply of axes the beginnings of a specialized industry had grown up round the flint-mining centres and in the trade of stone axes from the north and west of Britain to the purchasing centres of the south.

The elements of agricultural economy embodied in these British cultures had, in the first place, been acquired by the European barbarians, whose subsistence pattern had centred on food-gathering and the chase, from the centres of higher civilization in the Near East. But these regions had long been cognizant of the techniques of metallurgy when the first cultural borrowings of more easily assimilated ideas had led to the spread of agriculture across Europe among tribes still in a stone age, and on the heels of this first revolution in the technique of living came another—the production of metal from its natural ores and the fashioning of this new substance into tools and weapons. Early centres of metal-working grew up on the Continent where the trade routes from the Orient led to the necessary copper and tin ores for the production of bronze: routes by land, as into the Balkans and the Danube valley, or by sea towards the metal deposits of the Iberian Peninsula.

The builders of the great megalithic collective tombs of Spain and Portugal were already working in copper when people of a similar religion in western Britain were making almost identical tombs, but had lost or never known the arts of the metal-smith. A brilliant early metal age grew up in Spain: in Almeria, one of the centres of the collective - tomb people, the physical characteristics of the skeletons of the copper - workers suggest an actual Near Eastern immigration, and in central Spain there seems to have grown up a metal-using culture whose archæological remains can be equated with a distinctive physical type over the very large area eventually colonized by folk-movements from this region. These people, known from the characteristic pottery vessel so constantly buried in their graves as the Beaker folk, appear to have spread across France towards central Europe, bringing with them the knowledge of metallurgy, and recognizable themselves by their predominantly round-headed (brachycephalic) skulls, which suggest the Eastern Mediterranean as an ultimate point of origin. In the Rhineland one can trace the mingling of these people with the old native stock, and also with other arrivals—the Battle-axe people, whose ancestors had traversed the steppe country from south Russia to the Baltic and whose arrival in the north may have caused emigration across the North Sea to Britain of some of the constituents of the Peterborough group of people.

From Holland and the Rhineland the Beaker people invaded Britain in a succession of movements and landings spread over a century or so round about 1900–1800 B.C. The landings were mainly made along the east coast, from Kent and Sussex to Yorkshire, and again in Aberdeenshire; one group came in to Dorset and may have started from Brittany, where descendants of the Spanish Beaker folk had established themselves fairly early in the eastward spread of the culture. We shall see that the evidence suggests that at least the first landings were spear-heads of invasion, though certainly followed by a settlement phase, and the characteristics of the Battle-axe folk seem to have permeated the racially mixed Beaker invasion of Britain. Not only is there a clearly perceptible fusion of pottery styles and modes of burial, there is also an unmistakable hint of warrior chieftains imposing new ideas and planting new colonies of foreigners among the old neolithic stock.

For the Beaker invasion of Britain cuts across the whole complex of neolithic society as we can see it in the archæological record. There is the novel racial element—tall, heavy-boned, rugged, and round-headed —and there is an organization of society which is reflected not in the custom of collective burial without much regard for the trappings of the corpses, but in single graves, often under conspicuous mounds, where a man may lie in the clothing and armament of life ready to reassume in the next world his individual personality and status. More than this, the Beaker people brought to England, as they had to other

European regions, the first knowledge of and demand for metal tools and weapons, even if at first actual metalsmiths did not set up workshops in the newly settled areas.

The maximum incidence of the Beaker invasion was in the Lowland Zone of Britain—the south-east—which, while an area of agricultural fertility, had no natural sources of metal ores. These lay to the west—the copper ores of Ireland and of Weardale, the tin of Cornwall— and there is no evidence of direct Beaker immigration to these regions, only a late and sporadic eventual colonization of west Britain after the south-east had been intensively settled, and there is even less evidence of Irish settlement. Two things seem reasonably clear, therefore, when we come to consider the presence of copper or bronze daggers, axes, or other tools in the areas of maximum Beaker settlement, mainly if not exclusively of types familiar in Ireland and Atlantic Europe, and not likely to have been brought by the new arrivals from the Rhineland. The first is that a practical knowledge of metallurgy in Ireland and west Britain generally must have been established before or contemporaneously with the arrival of the Beaker folk in eastern Britain, but hardly by them; the second is that adequate trade routes between the areas of production and the areas of purchasing power must have been worked out at an early stage in the Beaker settlement phase.

The second of these factors—the routes to the west— we have already seen as existing as part of the foreign-stone axe trade late in the neolithic and before the arrival of the first Beaker contingents: routes to Cornwall, to North Wales, and to north-west England from the good pasturage of the Wessex chalk and the Thames

Valley gravels. The first and more crucial factor in the case raises many points at present unsolved in British prehistory, and discussion had best be postponed until we have further considered the complex nature of the Beaker immigrations themselves.

The new colonists can be recognized from a very large number of burials (between six and seven hundred in Britain, and a few in Ireland) and a smaller number of habitation sites, in all of which the characteristic, well-made, reddish or buff pots, ornamented with zones or panels of fine impressed cord or a very distinctive notched technique, have been found. A consideration of the types of these vessels suggests a division into two main groups (one again divisible itself into two), and the associated metal and stone types in the tombs confirm the essential duality of the Beaker invasion of Britain. The current nomenclature of the pots still continues to use a nineteenth-century typology which implied a sequence we now know to be inverted, so we start with the makers of beakers of type B.

These pots, with a curved profile and zonal ornament, come nearest to the assumed Spanish prototypes (though equally found in the Rhineland), and with them in graves may be associated copper daggers held in the haft by a tang (characteristic of all European Beaker peoples), and little stone plaques which, strapped on the left wrist, protected it against the flick back of the bowstring. A sub-group of pottery has a distinctive Wessex distribution and may represent a Breton contribution to the complex (or the Breton pots may come from Wessex): the daggers may have been imported from that region, though at least one mould shows them to have been cast in Ireland. In general, however, the B

Beaker folk colonized the same areas of south-eastern
England as did the makers of A type pots described
below (and also made landings in eastern Scotland),
and the evidence of the submergence of the Essex coast
shows that this geological event occurred after the
arrival of the B folk, but before that of the A group.
This evidence for priority of arrival is confirmed by
archæological stratigraphy in eastern England.

The A Beaker invasion made its main impact on East
Anglia and Yorkshire, and certainly came from the
Rhineland area. The pots show panel as well as zonal
ornament and their profiles reflect the contribution of
the potters of the Battle-axe people. It is hardly surprising that stone battle-axes are in fact found in graves
with A beakers in Britain, and there are also daggers
with riveted-on hilts (a Mediterranean type), or copies
of these in flint. The evidence of physical anthropology
confirms these Battle-axe elements in the British Beaker
population, for a number of skulls from A Beaker graves
belong to a dolichocephalic type associated with this
culture on the Continent, but dissimilar from the old
neolithic long-headed stock of these islands.

In Scotland, apart from specific direct colonization
probably from Holland, and in other parts of north
Britain, the Beaker types are represented by degenerate
forms grouped together as type C—minute analysis can
assign these to ultimate B or A origins in many instances,
but their significance is clearly that of local degeneration
or of secondary colonization from England and Wales
after the first force of the invasions was spent.

The burial rite was inhumation for all groups (a few
exceptional cremations are known), and graves, dug into
the subsoil, may be without any covering mound and

either isolated or grouped into small cemeteries of up to about twenty graves, or may be under conspicuous round barrows or cairns. Such barrow-burial is characteristic of the Battle-axe element in the Beaker culture in Europe, and in the British tombs we find accessory ritual features such as circular ditches or stone settings, or wooden structures, and the use of stone-built cists.

Numerically, the actual metal objects found in graves with Beaker burials are very few. Of 650 or rather more graves known, four have yielded tanged copper daggers with B Beakers, and eight, riveted daggers with those of type A or C. Other metal types found with Beaker burials include copper or bronze awls (about a dozen or so in England and Wales), while ring-bracelets or broad armlets of bronze are known from a few graves, bringing up the total to about thirty objects. While there is no up-to-date collation of the whole Beaker material of Britain to work on, and figures must be approximate pending detailed research, the number of Beaker graves containing copper or bronze objects must be rather under 5 per cent. of the total. This figure is quite comparable with that for Holland, a convenient area for comparison, where slightly over 4 per cent. of Beaker graves had metal objects in them. We shall see that similar figures obtain for Early Bronze Age graves in Britain not directly attributable to the Beaker colonists, and that 5 per cent. seems a very good average, on available evidence, for the proportion of the population able to acquire copper or bronze in the earliest metal-using communities in England, Scotland, or Wales.

The Beaker folk were not the only group intrusive to the old neolithic stock that can be traced taking a part in the early development of metallurgy in Britain, and before we can discuss this extremely important phase in our prehistory we shall have to consider the problems presented by those who are known, again from a pottery type, as the Food-vessel people. But with whatever group or groups we are dealing, the ultimate problem remains the same—the relationship of the areas in the west containing the natural metal lodes, which must have been exploited on the spot by persons well knowing the requirements of metal-smiths, if not smelting and founding themselves, and those who seem to have been the first in Lowland Britain to appreciate the value of metal tools, and to stimulate their production by purchase. The old foreign-stone axe routes might lead towards Irish copper or direct to the Cornish tin areas (a Beaker chieftain was buried on Salisbury Plain with a splendid battle-axe of rose-pink Land's End granite); but without tin-streamers working there, or Irish tinkers already trading at North Welsh ports, the neolithic Peterborough folk or their immediate successors in the trade, however knowledgeable in greenstone, could hardly of themselves have discovered the complex techniques of metallurgy and ore prospecting. Perhaps we have for too long looked only at the front door of Britain—the invasion coast of the Lowland Zone, with the Beaker chieftains leading in the little fleets of canoes to East Anglian creeks and harbours—and forgotten that the longer sea-routes of the west, that had brought the neolithic colonists and builders of megalithic tombs from Iberia and Brittany to the Irish Sea, still led to the back door in the Highland Zone—a back door that so well might be a tradesmen's entrance!

Though metal tools and weapons reached many of the

main areas of Beaker colonization in England—Derby-shire, Yorkshire, Wessex—yet such areas of primary settlement as East Anglia suffered by the capture of the trade in more westerly regions, and bronze daggers were imitated in flint by the less fortunate Beaker chieftains in these parts. Mining for flint and the production of axes certainly continued after the advent of Beaker people in Sussex and Wiltshire, and in the latter county a mining village of rather flimsy hurdle-work huts, partly dug into the ground, was built and occupied by users of Beaker pottery on Easton Down near Salisbury. A few domestic sites are known elsewhere, in the Highland Zone with circular stone-built hut foundations, or on the coast in an almost mesolithic manner. Grain impressions on pottery show that barley was the staple crop, as it continued to be throughout the Bronze Age in Britain.

The graves beneath barrows and cairns, often conspicuous on the crest-lines of hills, show that men, women, and children were entitled to a form of individual burial that might be monumental in character. In the area of dense Beaker occupation in Yorkshire the proportions of the sexes (where ascertainable or recorded) are almost equal; several barrows cover the grave of a man, a woman, and a child, or of a man and woman. The burials lay on one side, lightly crouched in the natural posture of sleep, though sometimes forcibly bound into a tight bundle. One skull from Crichel Down in Dorset had been trepanned before death, following a practice known on the Continent; on another the pathological erosion of the bone affords one of the earliest known examples of the deficiency disease, rickets. The warrior status of many male burials is shown by the accompanying dagger of stone or bronze, or a battle-axe, and the archery implied by the wrist-guards already mentioned is also suggested by the barbed flint tips that survived from a sheaf of half a dozen arrows in more than one man's grave, while the hawks' heads found in a couple of male burials look like evidence of falconry. A few ornaments were also acquired from the Irish gold-fields: a young archer buried at Radley near Oxford was wearing gold ear-rings. There is evidence of finely woven fabric, not likely to be linen, as flax seems to have been hardly known in Britain until later in the Bronze Age, but more probably woven from the fibres of nettles—a technique and fabric which survived in Scandinavia until the last century.

The most striking monuments of the Beaker people in Britain are, however, neither domestic nor directly sepulchral. In many of the Dutch barrows, where the Battle-axe element in the Beaker culture is strong, there is evidence of complex circular structures built around the grave with upright wooden posts, which may sometimes belong to roofed buildings, sometimes to fences or settings of posts with a structural or ritual significance. In general terms there is evidence of a probable Battle-axe, rather than true Beaker, ancestry for such complicated adjuncts to the tomb. In Britain there is some evidence for similar if simpler structures in Early Bronze Age barrows (a couple of small square wooden 'mortuary-houses' are known as well, from Beaulieu in the New Forest), but what appears to be an insular development takes place, whereby an open circular sanctuary, occasionally dedicated by a burial but not primarily designed as a tomb, is enclosed by structures of earthwork, timber settings, or upright stones. We have already seen that some such monuments may be attributable to the Peterborough-Skara Brae group of late neolithic cultures, perhaps in pre-Beaker times.

These circular sanctuaries seem to fall into three main classes. The first consists of a ditched enclosure with a single entrance, with or without a setting of wooden posts within the earthwork ditch and bank. This type of monument is known in East Anglia (Arminghall near Norwich), at Dorchester in Oxfordshire, in Dorset, and at Gorsey Bigbury on Mendip in Somerset; in Wiltshire the well-known 'Woodhenge' belongs to this group, and near this the more famous Stonehenge seems to have been such a sanctuary in its earliest phase, when it consisted of a ditch, a bank, and the 'Aubrey Holes' holding timber uprights, and had as yet no stone structure. At Stonehenge in this first phase and in a group of similar though smaller sites near Dorchester (Oxon) cremation burials were made within the sacred area. The evidence for dating shows that some of these monuments belong to late neolithic cultures and may date from before the advent of the B Beaker folk, and the association of others with certain specialized types of A Beaker ware may stress their Battle-axe connexions.

The second group also has an enclosing bank and ditch, but with two entrances, diametrically opposed. None are known with timber uprights (though some of the many unexcavated examples might show they existed), but several have standing stones within the earthwork. Direct or inferential evidence associates the excavated monuments of this class with the A Beakers, and they are widely distributed from Wessex to Yorkshire, and in Scotland. Arbor Low in Derbyshire is one of the finest of these sites, though its stones are now all fallen.

There remains the third group, of very wide distribution and a variety of type which reflects multiple origins and dates. Free-standing circles of upright stones are frequent all over the Highland Zone of Britain, varying considerably in size, and some or many of them must belong to later phases of the Bronze Age rather than the Beaker period. But at Avebury in Wiltshire such circles seem to have been erected by the B Beaker folk (the sub-group possibly derived from Brittany, where comparable structures occur), and the associated double lines, or avenues, of stones (again known from Brittany, and in England at Stanton Drew in Somerset) were certainly put up by these people. At Avebury the great bank and ditch is demonstrably a later feature than the B Beaker constructions, and may therefore be attributed to our second class of monument, although with four instead of two entrances.

It is suggested that the ditched elements and the use of wooden posts are early features in this series of monuments, harking back to a stoneless lowland country, and probably to Holland and the Battle-axe element in the mixed Beaker culture there, and their inception in Britain may antedate even the main B Beaker invasions, since, as we have seen, they have some significant associations with the late neolithic grooved ware described in Chapter III. The double-entrance monuments, so often with contained stone circles (two single-entrance sanctuaries with stone circles only are known, both in the Highland Zone), are likely to be attributable to the A Beaker folk, and seem to contain two distinct traditions —the stone circle, proper to the Highland Zone and perhaps having one of its origins in the free-standing curbs round some passage-graves, or a development of the crescentic forecourt, and the earthwork, essentially Lowland. Can we then see in these impressive structures an indirect expression of that linking of Highland to Lowland Zone that the early metal trade implies? The stones and the ditches of Arbor Low in Derbyshire or the Devil's Quoits at Stanton Harcourt in the Upper Thames valley would then symbolize the fusion of east and west as clearly as the Irish metal-work in the graves of the Dutch or Rhenish invaders who lie grouped around the sacred centres of their cult.

Of the nature of this cult we can only guess by analogy that an open sanctuary is appropriate to a sky-god, and that some may have been planned in relation to a celestial phenomenon such as sunrise at the summer solstice. Woodhenge may have been a roofed temple of some kind, as may another site at Avebury, and the circular-house type which on the Continent is characteristic of the western cultures (including the Beaker folk) rather than those of central Europe, may well have played a part in deciding the formal plan of these monuments. But it is interesting that the simple stone circles of the British types are scarcely known on the European mainland outside Brittany, and the ditched sanctuaries as a group are a unique British phenomenon, and stand as a tribute to the inventive genius of our Early Bronze Age population.

We have already noticed, in passing, that there was another major component in the cultural make-up of Early Bronze Age Britain in addition to the Beaker invaders. The Food-vessel culture is still rather imperfectly understood, but is represented by a large

number of burials in stone cists or in graves under
barrows in Ireland, Scotland, and northern England,
notably in Yorkshire, accompanied by pottery vessels
of several interrelated types, the earliest of which (on
the grounds of typology and association) are largely
derivative from the old neolithic Peterborough potting
traditions, though containing other elements in which
Beaker styles may themselves play a part. The southern
extent of the culture is somewhat uncertain, for, as we
shall see, fresh intrusive movements into Wessex about
1500 B.C. confuse and mask the native elements which
were developing inland, but there is reason to think
that some form of the Food-vessel culture stretched
southwards to the shores of the English Channel. The
anatomical evidence for the physical type of the Food-
vessel people is extremely important, for we find a
brachycephalic skull as the invariable accompaniment
of the characteristic pots, and in the Irish series at
least these skulls are apparently most closely comparable
with those of the continental Beaker series which have
neither Battle-axe nor indigenous northern neolithic
traits incorporated. The possibility of an immigration
from Iberia to Ireland has therefore been suggested on
this evidence, but the specifically British type of pottery,
with its roots in the local neolithic cultures, makes
this difficult to accept, though some Irish and west
Scottish food-vessels seem to show Iberian styles of
ornament.

Although we know nothing certain about the Peterborough neolithic type, it may have included an element
of brachycephaly. But even so, the Food-vessel people
as a whole can hardly be regarded as of indigenous
stock, but contingents allied to the Beaker invasions and

arriving in eastern Britain seem the only alternative explanation, and no more easy to accept.

Chronologically the Food-vessel culture seems to run on immediately after the Beakers, and there are many graves in north Britain which, without pots to assign them to one or the other group, may belong to either or both, and present a very uniform picture of a homogeneous Early Bronze Age culture in these regions. But specifically Food-vessel types can be detected, as well as pots—an elaborate form of necklace, with several strings of beads spaced into crescent form by pierced plates, was made in jet and shale in Scotland, Yorkshire, and Derbyshire, and traded sporadically elsewhere: in Wessex we shall see the same form translated into amber. Parallel with these crescentic necklaces, and perhaps copying them, are the gold *lunulæ* of Ireland, exported to west Britain and to the Continent, as were distinctive types of bronze axes and, above all, copper and bronze halberds, of which Ireland and Spain seem to have been the twin centres of origin, probably not unconnected. In all this metal trade, it seems likely that the Food-vessel people were as much concerned as the Beaker folk, and perhaps more so.

There is an interesting piece of evidence which underlines this probable connexion. On the slabs of several stone cists containing Food-vessel burials in Scotland, and on others of unassigned Early Bronze Age types, as well as on living rock surfaces, are curious carvings usually referred to as 'cups and rings'. Now such carvings are also found in Ireland, quite distinct from the carving on the Boyne group of passage-graves we have already noted, and concentrated significantly in the neighbourhood of copper ore in Kerry and Wicklow, while outside the British Isles excellent parallels can be found in north-west Spain and north Portugal. Here then might be support not only for the possible Iberian origin of the physical type associated with Food-vessels in Ireland, but also for that early establishment of metal-working in Ireland which we have seen reason to postulate as a parallel and approximately synchronous event with the coming of the Beaker invaders to eastern Britain. Such a migration of prospectors and metal-workers from north Spain to Ireland might conceivably result in a dominant male type in the ethnic record, with the adoption of native pottery types and the women who were responsible for them, and a retention of the magic in which cup-and-ring carvings played so important a part. Conceivably, too, some of the builders of the Boyne series of passage-graves may not have been unaware of the use of copper and the glitter of gold. The English and Scottish rock-carvings seem indeed to contain elements derived from passage-grave art, which would imply that the Boyne tombs were at least partly contemporary with the British food-vessels.

On the Yorkshire Wolds and in Scotland the Food-vessel people grew barley, and in the former region at least herded sheep for their wool, which they wove into cloth. Burials in boats hewn from the solid tree trunk here and in Wales may reflect trading activities by sea and river, and all over the area of Food-vessel settlement, burials, though individual, might be grouped into cemeteries of cists or under one barrow.

One may gather, from the Yorkshire evidence, interesting glimpses of the composite Early Bronze Age culture of the wolds which grew up with the mixture of Beaker and Food-vessel elements. Between eight and

nine hundred burials are known, all inhumations, and
of these just over fifty had bronze objects with them—
comparable figures from the similarly mixed Scottish
population at this time are about five hundred and
twenty graves and less than thirty bronze objects, and
in both areas the proportion is near the 5 per cent.
of bronze-possessing individuals implied by the all-over
figures for the Beaker culture in Britain.

Certain features of dress can be discerned, in addition
to the presence of woven woollen fabric in plain weave
with worsted-spun yarn, and fine fabric, probably
nettle - linen. Both the Beaker and the Food - vessel
people wore clothing fastened with buttons in front
(the prototype of coat or waistcoat) in the tradition of
the Iberian west and the continental Beaker folk, and
the buttons have remained where the cloth has vanished
in many instances, forming an instructive contrast to
the sartorial habits of the central European and Scandinavian Bronze Age people, who wore cloaks fastened
with pins. One male burial from Yorkshire had a pair
of jet buttons nine inches apart at the outer side of each
ankle, suggesting some form of gaiters, and the female
hair fashion is indicated by the frequent bone pin found
behind the skull in women's graves, where it had once
secured the bun of back hair. Ear-rings of bronze or gold,
or jet ear-studs, were worn, sometimes by young men
but usually by women, and women also had frequently
buried with them the small bronze awl that perhaps
constituted part of their sewing equipment. The men
seem often to have been buried with their dagger
gripped in the right hand, and sometimes the precious
blade was wrapped in cloth or moss or bark for protec-
tion, or traces of a scabbard of leather can be detected,

with a bone hook for the girdle. It is interesting to note
two men with badly set fractured thighs, and another
whose hip had become dislocated to such a degree that
a new growth of bone had formed on the pelvis to receive
the head of the femur.

The Food-vessel contribution to the Early Bronze
Age must have been of no mean order, even if we are
unable at present to disentangle its origins and resolve
the antinomy of an apparently intrusive physical type,
and the equally novel ideas of metal-working, associated
with a pottery which is in all essentials of British neolithic derivation. The Peterborough contribution to the
culture must have been considerable, and can hardly
have been entirely on the distaff side, for it is impossible
to dissociate the opening up of the metal trade between
the Irish-West British regions of production and the
southern and eastern English purchasing centres from
the old foreign-stone axe routes, which we know to have
been in use before the coming of the Beaker invaders,
and apparently largely in the hands of the Peterborough
folk. Contact between any (still very hypothetical)
brachycephalic Iberian metal-smiths and the descendants of the Peterborough people can hardly have taken
place in Ireland, which the latter are not known to have
reached—Lowland Scotland is perhaps a more hopeful
region. Some strains in the Food-vessel culture, as seen,
classically, in Yorkshire for instance, must be of Irish
origin, and the connexion between the two regions
already established in the days of the Clyde-Carlingford
neolithic culture must not be forgotten, while the evidence
of moulds suggests that Food-vessel colonies in east
Scotland were carrying out their own bronze-founding.
Much of the export trade in Irish Early Bronze Age

metal-work to Scandinavia and north Germany seems to have passed through Yorkshire, and that the Food-vessel folk were middlemen at least in such trade within Britain itself seems clear. How far they can be claimed as the real founders of the British Bronze Age we cannot tell at present.

In southern England a fusion of the intrusive ethnic elements with the old neolithic stock seems to have taken place along parallel lines to the situation we have seen in Yorkshire or Scotland in the centuries around 1700–1500 B.C., but the insular development of the British Bronze Age was here invigorated by a localized invasion into Dorset from Brittany. The essentials of this invasion appear to have been the immigration of a relatively small group of warrior chiefs—an ' heroic ' aristocracy burying its dead with an impressive panoply of weapons and such precious metal as could be obtained. The Breton graves show such heroes well equipped with bronze axes, and daggers which are ultimately of south French or north Italian types, together with some silver objects. In Wessex the tombs of the relatives and de-scendants of these people contain similar axes and daggers, but there is also a remarkable quantity of gold ornaments, amber and jet necklaces, and other objects imported to Dorset and Wiltshire not only from the remoter regions of the British Isles, but from Scandinavia, central Europe, and the eastern Mediterranean.

Behind this barbaric swagger and the implications of far-flung trade to which we will return, there can be traced the native stock, whose pottery traditions were those of Peterborough and the Food-vessels. Such con-centration of wealth as we see in the Wessex culture

graves can only have been possible to a few, to members
of a ruling caste, to a dynasty establishing itself as its
chieftains carved out for themselves little principalities
among a prosperous land of peasant farmers, and used
the natural wealth of the grain and hides and wool of
Wessex as a trade medium to exchange against luxury
goods. Two graves at least look like those of local princes,
probably of the entrance phase of the conquest (for such
it must have been). Here the objects buried with the
dead include not only gold-hafted daggers, but also
sceptres, that of a Dorset chief at Clandon near Dorchester, with a head of jet studded with gold, and that
of his Wiltshire counterpart at Bush Barrow near Stonehenge, with its shaft inlaid with polished bone zigzag
rings. As the new rulers consolidated their power, inter-
marriage seems to have taken place between invaders
and invaded, and in the later graves the native tradition
as exemplified by cord-ornamented pots derived from
Food-vessel types became more pronounced: that there
was a strong Food-vessel element, probably in the female
line, is shown too by the crescentic necklaces so well
known in jet from women's graves of the Food-vessel
culture in north Britain, which in Wessex reappear in
the more costly amber which must have been imported
from the Baltic lands.

The amber trade from Jutland across Europe to the
head of the Adriatic Sea was one of the main arteries
of commerce in the Bronze Age—the ultimate purchaser
of much of the amber was Mycenæan Greece, and along
the trade route northwards came new ideas in metallurgy,
actual imports, and a general stimulus to the peasant
communities of central Europe. Perhaps it was by this
route that the Wessex chieftains acquired blue glazed

beads of Eastern Mediterranean manufacture; certainly they obtained decorative bronze pins from central Europe, and it is likely that bronze axes with side-flanges cast to stiffen the implement, which seem to compete in southern England against the more simple hammered Irish types, were also imported from this region. The influence of Mycenæ itself was perceptible even in Wessex, where certain techniques of gold-work seem inevitably attributable to the brilliant Bronze Age of Mainland Greece round about 1600–1500 B.C., and not only do the famous Shaft-graves contain probably Baltic amber, but a bronze halberd ultimately of Irish origin. The trade in halberds from Irish centres of manufacture across England and Scotland to the Continent seems to date from this time, for miniature pendants representing these parade weapons occur in Wessex culture graves.

The chronological implications of this trade confirm those suggested by the crescentic amber necklaces (parallel to gold *lunulæ* and their jet counterparts in the Highland Zone) and the decorated bronze axes of Irish origin found in certain Wessex hoards of bronze tools and weapons, including the types of dagger that occur in the graves. On the Continent, the links with the central European Bronze Age already mentioned, and the known date of the blue glazed beads in the Near East, combine with the British evidence to suggest that this Wessex culture flourished between 1500 and 1200 B.C., with a survival into later centuries when its features become less and less distinctive, as the native traditions, based ultimately on Food-vessel origins, reassert themselves and absorb the intrusive elements.

Outside Wessex, the centre of the power of the Breton

dynasties, colonies can be traced in East Anglia, linked by the line of the Icknield Way, and in South Wales, and there is some likelihood of a metal-trade route between Ireland and Wessex which touched on this latter region and continued along the Mendips into Wiltshire. Here, at a time which seems likely to mark the culmination of Wessex power in Bronze Age Britain —power in the political sphere, and also in the spiritual, since the now prevalent rite of cremation seems to have replaced the earlier inhumation customs, in southern England at least, largely as a result of the Breton conquest of Wessex—a very remarkable architectural monument was erected. The ancient shrine of Stonehenge, probably by that time at least five hundred years old, and its timber uprights long rotted away, was rededicated, and a great central structure was built in stone, with uprights and lintels that betray in their craftsmanship the wooden prototypes of which they were gigantic copies. The larger stones are sarsens from twenty miles away, but the smaller uprights are of stones from the Presely Mountains in Pembrokeshire, transported by some great forgotten act of piety by a route that may have been that along the Mendips already mentioned. The A Beaker folk had reached South Wales and made battle-axes of the same Presely stone centuries before, and whatever was the route whereby the Blue Stones reached Stonehenge, it must have been in existence long before it was used for this remarkable feat of civil engineering.

Around Stonehenge, and again in the Avebury region of north Wiltshire and in southern Dorset, are grouped, often in remarkable concentration, specialized types of burial mounds in which considerable attention was paid to the formal external appearance of the structure, which instead of being a simple, bowl-shaped mound becomes a carefully built conical pile encircled at a short distance from the base by a precisely cut and accurately circular ditch. These bell-barrows, and related types such as the disc-barrow where the circular ditch becomes the main feature, with the burial mound reduced to a small central tump, are seen by their contained grave-goods to belong to the Wessex culture of the Bronze Age and to form one of its outward and visible expressions. In addition to the concentrations mentioned above, which seem to form clusters around sanctified spots or actual shrines, such types of burial mound, easily recognizable by field-work alone, have been shown to have a limited distribution almost exactly conterminous with the Wessex culture as known from other evidence. Not least interesting is the group of such barrows in East Anglia, where a Wessex culture colony seems to have been established at the northern end of the Icknield Way.

In some areas, notably that around Stonehenge and in the Middle Thames, it is possible to define barrow-groups which seem to constitute regular cemeteries, where the evidence of the contents of the graves shows that there has been a continuity of sanctity from Beaker times onwards through into the Middle Bronze Age. We can only guess at the territorial or dynastic heritage that may have lain behind the right to add barrows to one group rather than another: in the Stonehenge region at least it is likely that the high sanctity of the place brought funeral processions from long distances, and the New Forest sphagnum moss wrapping the dagger-blade of one Wessex culture chieftain buried there shows that he at least was an outlander from the other side of the Wiltshire Avon.

Beyond the limits of the Wessex dominion and its colonies, one can trace the presence of 'heroic' graves among the population that cannot in many regions (as in Scotland for instance) be regarded as directly of Wessex origin. We may have, rather, an indication of an internal social evolution comparable to that in Brittany itself which produced the Wessex invaders. The type of society favourable to the emergence of a warrior aristocracy has evolved in many places and at many times, and Heroic Ages may be found in Greece and Scandinavia separated by a millennium, while in prehistoric Britain we shall encounter a very similar aristocracy to that of Bronze Age Wessex in the Celtic Iron Age of the first couple of centuries B.C.

Over almost all Britain there grew up, parallel with the intrusive and mixed Wessex culture, and surviving it, a Middle Bronze Age culture known to us mainly from a large number of cremation burials, frequently under barrows or cairns, though in the north particularly being sometimes grouped into cemeteries without conspicuous covering mounds. Typically, such cremation burials are contained in a large pottery vessel or urn, and the Urn culture has been proposed as an inclusive term for this apparently homogeneous culture wherever it appears in Britain. Its origins seem basically in the Food-vessel culture, in which antecedents for the pottery types, and both barrow and cemetery burials, can be found. But cremation is not orthodox in such an ancestry, and this rite must rank as a new element, unless it be regarded as a result of an evolution of burial beliefs parallel with that on the Continent, where cremation also supersedes inhumation after the Early Bronze Age. In the Wessex culture, however, it is definitely intrusive, and here are associated with cremation burials little ritual pottery vessels, highly ornamented and recognizably derived from late neolithic Breton pottery styles, which, it has been conjectured with some reason, may have held the sacred ember used to light the funeral pyre.

Now with a great number of Urn culture burials, even in remote parts of north Britain, similar ritual vessels occur (one from Northumberland, incidentally, is a debased but clearly recognizable copy of a specifically Wessex culture type), and it is difficult to dissociate them from an ultimate origin in the south. But we must remember that cremation of a sort was practised by the neolithic people of Yorkshire, in chambered tombs in Ireland, and in other late neolithic contexts to which attention has already been drawn: so the final complete adoption of cremation as the burial rite all over Britain in the Middle Bronze Age (say by about 1200 B.C.) is unlikely to be entirely the result of permeation of novel religious ideas from Wessex.

Cremation robs us of much potential evidence from graves, though articles deposited unburnt with the burnt body do occasionally give us some light on chronology and culture. The blue glazed beads originating in the Near East about 1380 B.C. appear, perhaps by now as heirlooms, and amber and jet continue to be worn for ornaments. The rededication which we saw taking place at Stonehenge under the Wessex culture seems also to have been carried out at other ancient sacred circular monuments in several regions, from the Thames Valley to Scotland: the religious continuity implied in such ceremonies is important, and is another aspect of the cultural inheritance from the dawn of the Early Bronze Age implied by the potters' tradition in the urns. And actual continuity of structure can be seen too, as at Bleasdale near Garstang in Lancashire, where an elaborate wooden circular monument was built in the period of the Urn culture round a grave containing cremated burials in appropriate pots, but entirely in the Early Bronze Age tradition. Other less spectacular wooden circles within barrows are known from other regions, such as South Wales and in Dorset, carrying on the same ritual traditions into the Middle Bronze Age. There were clearly funeral rituals of great complexity observed in the construction and dedication of many of these barrow burials, and the trampled ground surfaces detected by skilled excavation in some sites give more than a hint that dancing may well have played its part at the funeral.

The widespread introduction of cremation among the Bronze Age tribes may not improbably have contributed to the forest clearance that growing agricultural demands with an enlarging population would make, for a human body needs a great deal of wood for its funeral pyre if cremation is to be as thorough as was that of Bronze Age Britain. Such pyres do not seem to have been on the site of the barrow as a rule, though one barrow in Wiltshire appears to have been thrown up over the remains of the pyre, with alternate layers of charred logs still lying at right angles to each other. Of the life of the Middle Bronze Age people we know little, as settlements have not yet been identified, but barley was grown, and what seem to be cattle-enclosures with earthwork banks and ditches are known from Somerset and the Berkshire

Downs, while stone-walled 'pounds' on Dartmoor and elsewhere may also be the work of the Urn culture, as may many groups of 'hut circles' in the same areas. There is no evidence of the use of the plough, and some form of hoe-cultivation is suggested by the irregular 'fields' associated with huts in Dartmoor that may be Middle Bronze Age.

It is clear that the traditions of the Middle Bronze Age cultures mainly known to us from the urn burials must have had a very long survival in the Highland Zone, in the remoter parts of which it is exceedingly difficult to make any sort of a chronological equation with regions where the sequence of cultures can be brought into relationship with the more precisely defined European time-scale. In such regions as Scotland, and often in Ireland, cultures formally derivative from Middle Bronze Age traditions have to be studied almost in isolation, and constitute a distinctive group of Late Bronze Age cultures within the Highland Zone almost unaffected by the immigrant movements which we shall see taking place in southern England from about 900 B.C. onwards, which introduced novel forms of agricultural economy as well as metal types, and heralded the coming of iron as a cheap tool-metal. In the Highland Zone the Late Bronze Age survived until the local appearance of iron-using peoples, perhaps several centuries after their establishment in the Lowland Zone.

Numerous cremation cemeteries, or burials under barrows and cairns, show the persistence and degeneration of types of pottery going back to Middle Bronze Age prototypes, in which the strongly defined divisions of rim, collar, neck, and shoulder become vestigially represented by cordons of applied clay round a barrel-shaped pot. These Cordoned Urns represent one side of the Highland Zone Late Bronze Age tradition, and with them, too, other types with applied plastic ornament, possibly of Iberian Bronze Age inspiration, or perhaps a recrudescence of native traditions of encrusted ornament going back to the late neolithic styles of Skara Brae. But for much of our information about the Late Bronze Age in the west and north we have to turn to the specialized products of the metal-smiths, which can rarely be equated with much certainty with the evidence from the cemeteries.

The natural copper deposits of Ireland and Scotland ensured the Highland Zone a continued dominance in the metal industry and trade after the brilliant start made in the early second millennium. The individuality of the British smiths, no less than their technical skill, is seen in a whole succession of rapier and spear types and the development of the flat and flanged axe into a narrow form known as a palstave. These tools and weapons were not only sure of a sale within these islands, but were exported to a ready market in northern Europe from Spain to Scandinavia. A circular, targe-like shield seems to have been a British Highland Zone invention: it is known in wood and in leather, the latter type being apparently made by pressing the wet skin into a prepared wooden mould which would give the required features of concentric ribs and a central boss over the hand-grip. In metal, such shields are often superbly made and up to three feet across, with a ribbed and bossed surface strongly suggesting a wooden, nail-studded prototype, and seem to have been exported to the Continent and there to have given rise to various imitations and similar forms.

There was much coming and going of metal traders between Scandinavia and Ireland in the Late Bronze Age, and it is likely that a trick of ornament on bronze and gold work consisting of fine concentric circles drawn with a compass is of Danish or North German origin, though of frequent occurrence on Irish gold and bronze objects. Gold-plated bronze discs ornamented in this manner seem to have been exported from Ireland, and are likely to be associated with some form of sun-worship, for in Denmark one such disc was mounted on a bronze model of a horse and a four-wheeled chariot, strongly suggestive of such an interpretation. The contemporary heavy bronze neck ornaments of Scandinavia were copied in gold in Ireland—all this trade must have involved considerable shipping, and large sea-going vessels are indeed shown on Scandinavian rock-engravings, which in one instance also include a man with a British circular shield on his arm. In Wales, a wooden bowl was found which is really a model boat, oval in plan and with applied gold - leaf decorated with multiple compass-circles arranged in a manner strangely like the rows of shields on the gunwales of Viking ships, beneath which incised gold - filled zigzags suggest stylized waves, while at the prow and stern are two oval 'eyes', following an ancient practice among primitive shipbuilders. And with this may be taken a remarkable little model of a longboat in wood, in which stand carved warriors holding round shields and having fierce eyes of inlaid quartz, found in East York-shire, which has rather better claims to be regarded as Late Bronze Age (on continental evidence) than as Viking, following the orthodox view in this country.

In Denmark fine trumpets of bronze were evolved in the Late Bronze Age, but while these may have influenced some of the later Irish examples, there seems to have been an independent creation of a bronze trumpet in the west, the forms of which imply enlarged bronze versions of a cow's horn. Very large instruments of this type were made with great skill, some being blown from the end and some from the side, and must have contributed in no small degree to the terror and confusion created by the war-bands of the time. The slashing sword, which as we shall see was invented in central Europe, and was at this time spreading across the European continent in the hands of warriors, does not seem to have reached the Highland Zone of Britain until an advanced stage of the Late Bronze Age, though it did eventually arrive to compete with the older rapier, either with raiding bands or more probably as the result of trade, and was copied and cast by the local metal-smiths. The western sea-routes brought to Britain occasional objects of bronze-work that can be recognized as of types current in Europe in what, by about 600 B.C., was the full flower of the earlier phase of the Iron Age there—a knobbed necklet in North Wales, ring-decorated necklets and a bronze bowl with incised ornament from western Scotland, indicate a trickle of trade still continuing. How near to the Iron Age even western Britain was becoming is shown by the great hoard of household gear found, apparently abandoned by a raider, in a mountain lake in South Wales, but by its richness clearly the original property of a prosperous man of the Glamorganshire plain—a hoard which in addition to its bronze types of British Highland Zone derivation contained an iron sword characteristic of the Hallstatt

Iron Age of continental Europe, and other iron objects probably locally manufactured.

Among the objects in this hoard must be mentioned two great cauldrons made of sheets of riveted bronze, and each with two ring-handles by which they could be suspended by a double-branched pot-hook of the type known from the continental Iron Age cultures. These cauldrons are of Irish manufacture, and the ultimate origin seems to have been in the *deinos* of the Greek world, which from trading-stations such as that of Massilia (Marseilles) founded about 600 B.C., or Ampurias, farther west, would have reached the western Mediterranean and the Atlantic coast sea-ways during the British Late Bronze Age. Such cauldrons (with accompanying flesh-hooks for picking out the seethed meat) became firmly established as a feature of west British and Irish prehistory. The cauldron as the symbol of chieftainship and hospitality is a frequent *motif* in the Irish sagas of the Dark Ages that reflect the old pre-Christian western Celtic world, and Welsh tradition remembered in its medieval tales the men who had brought these great vessels across the seas from Ireland to Wales. In the South Welsh hoard, the two cauldrons look like the workmanship of one man, and the wear on the rims and handles shows the rubbing of a flat surface, only explained by storage upside down on a shelf or table, and giving an unexpected and intriguing glimpse of the furnishings of a Late Bronze Age chieftain's house.

A less substantial household is reflected in the finds from a cave at Heathery Burn in Co. Durham, which had been inhabited in the Late Bronze Age by a family or group which included bronze-smiths who were using the Weardale copper ores. The reasons which drove these people to live in such dark and damp conditions are obscure in detail, but less so in the general picture of Late Bronze Age Britain, where the very numerous hoards of bronze-smiths' scrap, and sometimes the worker's stock-in-trade of tools, buried at some crisis in the hope of eventual recovery but never reclaimed, hint at a time of troubles, of uncertainty and of raiding war-bands. This insecurity is confirmed by increasing developments in armaments. In the Heathery Burn cave were the cheek-pieces for horses' bits, and four bronze nave-bands which suggest a four-wheeled cart in the manner of those of the Hallstatt Iron Age of the Continent and are the earliest evidence of a wheeled vehicle in this country.

An even more desperate impression of fugitive metal-workers, however, is that given by finds in the remote Shetlands, where a metal-smith, trained in the Irish schools of his craft, set up a smithy and foundry in a croft or tiny hamlet of two or three houses on Sumburgh Head. The community in which he settled had been formally in a Stone Age, so far as the archæological evidence can tell us, up to the time of his arrival, at some undetermined date that is not likely to be before the fifth or sixth century B.C. Barley had been grown, and cattle kept, and in fact a stall with a whale vertebra as a tethering ring fixed into the wall had a paved, dished floor implying the collection of manure—the first known instance of this in prehistoric Britain. Fish and shell-fish were eaten, and the whole economy was closely comparable to that of the late neolithic site of Skara Brae in Orkney. Who bought the Irish smith's swords, knives, pins, and axes, and with what medium of barter? In this tiny, poverty-stricken community there can have been little demand or little to offer for such costly objects as leaf-shaped slashing swords, yet such were undoubtedly cast there and presumably disposed of. There is some iron slag from the smithy, and though the metal types cast were those of the Late Bronze Age, the actual date of such a curiously isolated workshop might be well after the adoption of iron in more favoured regions.

Elsewhere in the Highland Zone similar long survivals of Late Bronze Age cultures are suggested, if less dramatically presented than the Shetland evidence. In Ireland itself an ultimate Bronze Age may well survive to 200 B.C. or even later, and to the coming of Iron Age invaders into Ulster. But to a period which should be contemporary with the main Late Bronze Age of Britain (i.e. not much later than 500 B.C.) may be attributed a settlement at Ballinderry, where the timber-work of a large rectangular house, 40 by 45 feet, on a curious carpentered foundation framework of mortised beams and against one side of a palisaded enclosure, was preserved in a peat-bog. Within the palisade were also a number of small, circular, wattle-lined pits which seem to have been for grain storage rather than any form of habitation, and which recall similar grain-pits in the southern English Iron Age. As we shall see, there is something comparable in the Late Bronze Age in Kent, though here associated with evidence of an immigrant culture of European origin. The evidence which, it is claimed, would place a circular fort of the 'rath' class at Cush within the Late Bronze Age does not seem wholly satisfactory, and would, if accepted, bring the survival of such a culture to the first century B.C. or later.

In the Highland Zone of Britain these ultimate descendants of the Middle Bronze Age cultural traditions
were living relatively untouched by the happenings
on the Continent, save for the importation of some
novel types of bronze tools and weapons, while still
successfully competing in foreign markets with some of
their own products. There is evidence, however, from
several regions, such as north-east Scotland, Yorkshire,
and Ireland, that some immigrant peoples making a
new type of pottery (sometimes known as 'Flat-rimmed
Ware') may have been forming settlements in these
regions, and the characteristic pottery suggests a possible
origin in north-west Germany. The south-east corner
of the Lowland Zone was at about the same time as
this, or earlier, receiving immigrants from across the
Channel as a result of the disturbed conditions resulting
from the movements of peoples from central Europe.
Round about 1000 B.C. there had grown up a distinctive
Late Bronze Age culture in this region which, as we
have seen, counted among its achievements the development of the slashing sword and an increased use of the
horse as a riding animal—two features which together
constituted a formidable technological advance in the
art of warfare, and can hardly have been without their
effect in the rapid expansion of these peoples which
the archæological record attests. No less distinctive than
their swords were the cremation cemeteries or urnfields
which provide evidence of various local varieties of this
Late Bronze Age culture of Europe, and the spread of
the Urnfield folk westwards into France and ultimately
to Spain is a well-attested event spread over several
centuries.

It is only to be expected that the pressure of these

folk-migrations, probably not unaccompanied by war-like raids, had its effect on the indigenous Middle Bronze Age folk in France; and from the region of Picardy, where such a retarded culture had survived, we can trace a small colony of emigrants settling in Thanet about 900 B.C. More extensive colonization from northern France, however, can be detected at about this time in Sussex, where on the downland between Lewes and Brighton actual farmsteads and fields have been identified, and constitute the earliest examples so far known in Britain of field-systems of a type which persist until, and during, the period of the Roman Occupation. The partial excavations in the Sussex sites show that the farm lay-out included roughly oval or sub-rectangular banked enclosures with one or more entrances, within which were timber structures which may have been for storage or habitation and were perhaps sometimes circular in plan: some post-holes discovered, however, may not have supported roofed buildings at all. Associated with these enclosures was a system of small rectangular fields, their outlines revealed, where they run parallel to the contours on the hillside, by the soil-creep to the lower edge of the field which results from continued ploughing, and between the fields farm-tracks or roadways were similarly defined. Evidence of occupation consisted of pottery fragments, the styles of which relate the settlers to the Middle Bronze Age folk of northern France, dispossessed by the Urnfield invaders from their ancestral territory, clay spindle-whorls showing that spinning and presumably weaving were among the household crafts, and a couple of whet-stones, chemical analysis of the surface of which provided a telling foreshadowing of things to come—evidence that iron tools had been whetted on them. Too rare and precious to be left behind like some of the broken bronze tools found among the household debris, these first iron objects in Britain are known only by inference.

The use of iron as a cheap, easily obtainable, and eminently satisfactory metal for tools and weapons was already becoming known on the European continent after its discovery, probably before 1500 B.C., in the Near East, perhaps in Anatolia. The first iron-using cultures grew up in central Europe on the foundation of the Late Bronze Age Urnfield traditions, and the spread of the Urnfield folk across Europe had prepared the way for a very rapid spread of the new techniques of blacksmithing, as well as actual fresh movements of people, now armed with iron swords. Some of the Urnfield territories in the west, themselves the result of immigration and probably conquest from east of the Rhine, now felt the onslaught of warrior bands from the colonists' own remote homeland, and in the west Alpine region, where a brilliant Late Bronze Age culture had grown up round the margin of the Swiss lakes, the coming of iron-using people of the Hallstatt Iron Age culture about 750 B.C. resulted in a part of the population emigrating and seeking fresh territories in northern France and beyond. Trade contacts between Britain and the west Alpine regions may have existed before this time, for imported types of bronze swords, axes, and other objects in southern England, all of west Alpine origin, are relatively abundant, but that there must have also been some actual immigration of people is shown by farmsteads, probably dating between 750 and 500 B.C., that were set up near those of the earlier arrivals from north France on the Sussex Downs at Plumpton Plain near Brighton.

Here the same type of fields seem to have been ploughed as those of the first arrivals, and though no embanked enclosures were made, post-holes suggest wooden structures similar to those on the earlier farm. The pottery has traces of its west Alpine ancestry, and a broken bronze axe confirms this origin, while half a dozen whetstones showed the tell-tale traces of iron. Another Late Bronze Age agricultural settlement likely to be of the same origin was found on the foreshore at Birchington in Kent: in its earliest phase circular grain-storage pits and shallow 'working-places' probably connected with threshing-and-winnowing were in use, characteristic of farming methods in the British Early Iron Age of some centuries later, and the second phase at Birchington had evidence of timber and hurdle-work buildings preserved by waterlogging. The same cause led to the preservation of much vegetable debris which included the seeds of many weeds of cultivation, implying arable fields near by. At Brentford, again, a west Alpine settlement seems to have existed on the banks of the Thames.

At both sites at Plumpton Plain the pottery types distinctive respectively of the north French Middle Bronze Age and of the west Alpine Late Bronze Age cultures were found mixed with coarse wares ornamented with applied bands of clay and much surface decoration made by impressing the finger-tips. Such ware has its origins in late neolithic cultures of the end of the third millennium B.C. in northern and western Europe from Holland to Spain, and represents the strong survival of ancient traditions there throughout the Bronze Age.

In the English Late Bronze Age, however, such pottery is intrusive, but beyond Sussex is widely distributed over southern England from Wessex to East Anglia, often in urnfields of cremated burials. This characteristic type of burial shows that the immigrant culture, which must have entered Britain some time around 750 B.C. or a little later, has a strong Urnfield element in its continental ancestry, and indeed it appears to be the result of a fusion of Urnfield and older stocks at many places along the north European seaboard. It is noticeably well developed in Holland, whence some of the British groups may well have come by the same cross-Channel routes and to the same landfalls as the Beaker folk a thousand years before, while others may have crossed over to the Dorset coast from points farther down the Channel seaboard. In eastern England this culture is almost exclusively represented by cemeteries, but in Wessex and Sussex (thanks to more vigorous archæo-logical field-work and excavation) settlement sites are known, as well as field-systems and earthwork enclosures for cattle-pounding and other agricultural purposes.

In southern Dorset the Late Bronze Age urnfields may contain up to a hundred burials, and cremation burials may also occur under barrows—a tradition common to the English Middle Bronze Age and to the coeval cultures in Europe. From one such barrow burial (the Deverel Barrow) and from a cemetery in this region (Rimbury near Weymouth) the name Deverel-Rimbury has been coined for this distinctive culture. As well as flat cemeteries or urnfields, and burials under barrows specifically erected in the Late Bronze Age, Deverel-Rimbury burials were also often inserted in the mounds of Middle or Early Bronze Age barrows, usually

tending to be restricted to a quadrant or arc towards
the south or south-east, while small cemeteries have been
found where the urns are arranged in a circle. This
tradition of circle-veneration seems likely to come from
native Middle Bronze Age sources, and recalls the late
neolithic or Early Bronze Age circular shrines with peri-
pheral cremation burials which we have already noticed.
In the Deverel Barrow itself the burials were placed at
the foot of massive stones arranged in a horseshoe plan,
again reminiscent of earlier traditions.

On the chalk downs of Dorset and Wiltshire it has
been possible to identify quite considerable earthwork
enclosure banks and ditches which delimit large areas
of land in the manner of estate or tribal boundaries,
and are referable to the Deverel - Rimbury culture.
These Late Bronze Age land-divisions are of considerable
interest as the first known examples in Britain, and
probably in northern Europe, which enclose more than
the immediate surroundings of a farm or hamlet, for
they demarcate areas which can only be compared with
cattle ranches, with bank-and-ditch boundaries which
would serve to keep the beasts from straying into the
arable fields and along the flat-bottomed ditches of
which cattle could be driven from one area to another.
In one region north of Salisbury a system of boundaries
almost certainly all of Deverel-Rimbury date can be
traced on the high ground on both sides of the valley
of the River Bourne. The intense occupation and agriculture in the valley itself since medieval times has in
many instances destroyed the lower ends of the Late
Bronze Age ditches that outline long strips, averaging
three-quarters of a mile wide, along the valley, and with
lengths that, running from river to hill-crest, would have

been about two miles, but the pattern of these parallel units of land (probably at least six placed side by side can be traced at one point) is as a whole clear. It is tempting to draw a parallel with the Saxon land-divisions and later parish boundaries in many of the Wessex chalk-land areas, where such an allocation on the valley-side gave a fair proportion of hill pasture and water meadows to each strip.

The picture of large-scale pastoralism suggested by these land-divisions can be filled out by the evidence of actual farmsteads and smaller earthwork enclosures. At the southern end of the group of 'ranches' just described, on Thorny Down, the post-structure of a timber-built house, oblong and about 25 by 15 feet, with a door and a porch on one long side and probably an inner partition into two rooms, was found in its farmyard. This included other buildings, one also rectangular but smaller than the main house, and another probably a circular store-shed, while other groups of close-set posts presumably held granaries or similar structures clear of the ground. Barley was certainly grown by the Deverel-Rimbury folk, for in one of the post-holes of a timber structure (perhaps a granary) elsewhere in Wiltshire (near Wood-henge) actual grains of this cereal were found.

In Sussex on New Barn Down near Worthing another steading was partially excavated and contained at least two circular timber-built structures, though neither need be the main farmhouse: here the farmyard was sur-rounded by a wooden-post fence and a bank and ditch, to which an approach road ran, between the small rectangular fields about 250 feet wide and of uncertain lengths, and thus showing the essential contemporaneity of the whole lay-out.

Something closely related to the small earthwork enclosures of the type already noted on the earlier site at Plumpton Plain is also known from the Wessex Deverel-Rimbury area, though not so far identified in the south Dorset region, where the large urnfields no less than the geographical proximity to the coast suggest the primary settlement area of the immigrants. The enclosures may possibly have native Middle Bronze Age ancestors in the Berkshire and Somerset sites already mentioned, or may have reached Wessex from Sussex by an inland route. However that may be, there are in north Wiltshire, and again on Salisbury Plain and in Cranborne Chase farther south, a number of enclosures that vary in plan between irregular ovals and sub-rectangular forms, and which may in some instances at least have been used as pastoral enclosures rather than as settlement sites. The V-section of the ditches of these enclosures and of the boundary ditches marks a change from the tradition of wide flat-bottomed ditch-digging that is characteristic in the English chalk areas from neolithic times throughout the Early and Middle Bronze Age, and the new steep-sided, narrower form comes to persist through the ensuing Iron Age, when it was admirably adapted to the construction of fortifications. At one Deverel-Rimbury site in Dorset the broken bronze spud used to dig the ditch was found discarded in the rubble at the bottom, and fitted the tool-marks that could still be seen on the chalk sides of the ditch.

In the cemeteries it was very exceptional for any object to be buried with the dead, and so we have relatively little information on the possible trade contacts of the Deverel-Rimbury folk with regions outside their own territory. Bronzes from settlement sites and certain

pottery styles indicate contacts with the west in all likelihood not unconnected with the exploitation of the tin
ores of Cornwall, while connexion with the western
seaboard of the Continent at this time is shown by imports of types of bronze axes peculiar to Brittany and
Spain respectively, both of which were traded into
south-west England. Spear-heads which represent a
native Bronze Age form developing under foreign
stimulus were used in the Deverel-Rimbury culture and
are common elsewhere in Britain, especially in Ireland,
where they seem to have mainly been manufactured.
Moulds for such spears from Argyllshire, however, show
that Scotland too was actively concerned in the trade, and
as on the back of one of these is the matrix for casting the
type of bronze razor frequently found with the Cordoned
Urns in that region, we have an interesting chronological
link between Highland and Lowland zones, and an
indication that the Cordoned Urn culture may have
been flourishing at about 600 B.C. In Wessex, the razors
used by the Deverel - Rimbury men (though never
buried with them) belong to a type dissimilar from that
mentioned above, and must be foreign imports from
the Continent—they were in fact traded far beyond the
limits of the Deverel-Rimbury culture and well into the
Highland Zone to compete with the old native form.

The cultural innovations associated with these immigrant Late Bronze Age moves into southern England
were to prove of very great importance in the subsequent
development of British agriculture and rustic industry.
The rectangular fields implying the use of an ox-drawn
plough denote a real revolution in agriculture, and an
enormous potential increase in food production over
the older hoe-cultivation which we must believe to have

continued in Britain until this time, in the absence of
any concrete evidence to the contrary. Ploughing with
ox-teams of two, four, or six beasts is attested for earlier
phases of the Bronze Age in Europe by rock-engravings
in Scandinavia and the maritime Alps, but there is no
evidence of the ox-drawn plough in Britain before the
field-systems of the Plumpton Plain settlements. The
agricultural economy which used such fields was shared
by the Deverel-Rimbury folk, and once established in
Sussex and Wessex it continued to be employed by
the later occupants of the earliest iron-using cultures
in those regions, themselves originating in the same
areas of northern France as our Late Bronze Age immigrants. The iron on the whetstones from Plumpton
Plain settlements shows that even in the first phase of
our Late Bronze Age this metal was in use by a favoured
few at least, and a piece of iron slag in a Deverel-Rimbury
site in Wiltshire points in the same direction. The
immigrant Late Bronze Age of southern England was
but the forerunner of the earliest Iron Age in the same
region, not only in the techniques of agriculture, but
almost certainly in terms of ethnic kinship. For we have
now come to a place in our prehistory when we can
with some assurance talk of the Celts, and the great
early Celtic expansion of the Continent is recognized
to be that of the Urnfield people, one of the main
formative elements in whose composition were the older
European Bronze Age cultures with barrow burial
which we have seen to have formed the vanguard of
our Late Bronze Age invasions. Earlier, 'proto-Celtic'
elements may have been a part of our more ancient
Bronze Age cultures, but from now on we are decisively
in a Celtic Britain.

CHAPTER V

THE IRON AGE

As we saw in the last chapter, the later phases of the British Bronze Age take the form of a series of immigrant cultures introduced from the Continent and cutting across the otherwise rather insular development that had gone on in this country since the beginnings of metallurgy in the second millennium B.C. These intrusive movements of peoples into southern England between about 850 and 700 B.C. were themselves the outcome of folk-migration and cultural changes on the mainland of Europe; and on the Continent the spread of the Late Bronze Age Urnfield cultures heralded the subsequent spread from central Europe, westwards and northwards, of the use of iron for tools and weapons. The relative abundance of iron ore, and its wide distribution, contrasts with the localized deposits of copper and tin, and the possibility of a cheap and very efficient metal for tools and weapons inevitably made for modifications in the agricultural economy which had been developed in the Late Bronze Age by broadening the basis of prosperity beyond the limited number of persons or groups who could acquire the more expensive bronze. The social structure of the European Iron Age, then, is that of increasingly large numbers of farming communities—in Britain at least seemingly based on the farmsteads of individual families, rather than on village communities. These provided a stable and prosperous background against which we can see the emergence

of a warrior aristocracy comparable to that of the
Wessex Bronze Age, also favoured by conditions of an
agricultural economy sufficiently advanced to provide
some surplus wealth which could be used to encourage
fine craftsmanship in objects of adornment and warfare.
The insistent tribalism of the Celts gave every oppor-
tunity for a warrior caste, and, throughout the British
Iron Age, methods of attack and defence, weapons
and fortifications, form much of our material for
study.

The two major phases of the continental Iron Age,
those of Hallstatt and of La Tène, are of course based on
the older Bronze Age traditions and even those of earlier
times. Iron-using Hallstatt cultures grow up over a large
area centred in west Germany soon after 750 B.C., and
expand to reach westwards even to northern Spain—
an expansion partly caused by the increasing westward
pressure of Teutonic tribes from east of the Elbe in the
eighth century. Contacts with the classical world become
established late in Hallstatt times in the Rhône Valley
after the founding of the Greek colonies such as Massilia
early in the sixth century, but the decisive influence of
the Mediterranean comes with the Etruscan expansion
to Bologna and North Italy. From these regions wine
was exported across the Alps in the fifth century and,
as with the early European tea-trade with China, this
was accompanied by the export of objects of art, and
the Greek and Etruscan metal-work was profoundly to
affect the Celtic craftsmen. Elements added from the
Orient, and from the art of the Northern Nomads, combined with the old Hallstatt traditions and the new
classical *motifs* to form an art style which is characteristic of the La Tène phase, and which is perhaps the

major contribution of European prehistory to the artistic heritage of the world.

Britain could not be unaffected by these events in Europe. The Late Bronze Age immigrations into southern England had shown the way whereby displaced persons or exploratory war-bands might escape from a troubled Continent to an island which still offered opportunities for colonization or local conquests; contacts established between the two sides of the English Channel in the tenth century must still have been kept up by trade and probably actual movements of population until late in the fifth, when we can identify the arrival of the first iron-users in England.

A group of people of Lower Rhenish or Dutch origin landed in Yorkshire, where a settlement which may be as early as about 450 B.C. has been found at Scarborough, and other sites such as Harling in Norfolk may also date from before 400 B.C. Clearly individual landings were made by groups of diverse continental origins—in east Sussex pottery was being made near Folkestone with painted ornament in a manner characteristic of south-west Germany, but quite alien to the remainder of the British Iron Age; other groups show in their pottery indications of a Teutonic admixture in their otherwise Celtic make-up. Into Wessex came considerable drafts of population from the north French regions south of Paris about 400 B.C., and at about this time other areas in Northamptonshire and the Thames Valley were also settled.

In these various regions of southern and south-eastern England we have then, by soon after 400 B.C., a number of allied groups of Iron Age cultures established among the indigenous Late Bronze Age population, ultimately

of the same Celtic origin on the Continent, and likely
to have been speaking closely related dialects. The
various cultures, with local distinctions, but funda-
mentally homogeneous and of Hallstatt stock, have been
grouped for convenience as the Iron Age A culture of
Britain, and can be considered as a whole in any
discussion of their general features.

A large amount of material exists on which to base
our knowledge of Iron Age A, almost exclusively derived
from settlement sites, open or fortified. In Wiltshire,
where the culture has been extensively studied, the
characteristic economic unit seems to have been that of
the farmstead rather than the village, and this generaliza-
tion is probably true for the wider area of settlement,
though the existence of true villages is by no means
impossible. The hill-top fortifications (' camps ') of Iron
Age A, a few of which belong to the early (entrance)
phase, though most, as we shall see, are likely to have
been built in a time of sudden emergency in the middle
of the third century, appear on the available evidence
to have been for temporary refuge during tribal warfare
rather than for permanent or prolonged occupation,
though they seem to have been increasingly inhabited
from the third century onwards. Farming settlements
may, however, have existed within the ramparts in
times of peace in some, though not all, of these hill-
forts.

The agricultural techniques introduced in the Late
Bronze Age, and based on the use of an ox-drawn
plough which produces a rectangular field, were continued and developed by the Iron Age A people, and
indeed this system of farming continued among the
various Iron Age groups all over England until and into

the period of Roman occupation. Extensive systems of small rectangular fields outlined either by the earthen banks and the ' lynchets ' formed by soil-creep at their lower edges in the chalk-lands and allied terrain, or by stone walls in more rocky country, give abundant evidence of the corn-growing which, more than stock-breeding, seems to have been the main feature in the Iron Age farming economy. In addition to the staple Bronze Age crop, barley, there appear in the British Iron Age emmer wheat in relative abundance, as well as bread wheat, oats, and rye—the first appearance in British prehistory of the last cereal, which was to play such an important part as a bread grain throughout the Middle Ages.

The extensive excavation of an Iron Age A farmstead at Little Woodbury near Salisbury gives us a convincing picture which can be used as typical of a large number of other sites known only in part. The settlement, on a low bluff of downland three-quarters of a mile away from the nearest water supply, was enclosed by a roughly circular timber fence or palisade some 350 feet across, clearly not defensive against anything more than thieves and wild animals, and having a single gateway which seems to have been built with a certain amount of rustic pretension, and had a double gate closing on a central post which would have precluded the entry of carts. Opposite this entrance, and not far from the centre of the enclosure, stood the farmhouse, a strongly built wooden circular structure 45 feet in diameter, with a low-pitched conical roof, probably of turf, its rafters converging on four massive posts which stood at the angles of a central hearth. An entrance with a porch looked towards the gateway in the enclosure

fence, and the whole gives an impression of a solid
standard of barbarian comfort with sound carpentry
made possible no doubt by the improvements in tools
resulting from the use of iron.

The arrangements of the farmyard were of singular
interest, and their interpretation enabled a large number
of sites known from imperfect exploration in the past
to be understood. The outstanding feature was the
very large number of circular pits, from three to six
feet across and sometimes six feet in depth, and filled
with miscellaneous occupational debris—burnt soil and
stones, bits of clay daub, broken pottery, animal bones,
etc. Such pits had been known as a feature of Iron
Age sites in southern England for many years, and had
been explained as underground 'pit-dwellings', but
it was clear from a re-examination in the light of the
new knowledge that their primary purpose had been
for corn storage, and that subsequently they had been
used as convenient tips for rubbish, or the soil dug out
from new pits. Such corn storage is mentioned by
Diodorus Siculus as existing in Britain in his time, and
it is to-day still known in many regions of Europe (e.g. in
some south Italian towns grain is stored in circular
vaults beneath the market-places). Infection from mildew
or other causes may cause a pit to become unfit for
further use, and consequently, in a settlement of long
duration, a large number of pits will be dug and refilled,
though only a few are in use for any one harvest. In the
Wiltshire site in question, it was estimated that the
settlement had had a life of some three centuries, and
at the end of that time about 360 pits had been dug;
and at a generous estimate of a life of ten years for a
pit, not more than a dozen need have been open at

once, with a storage capacity of about fifty-five bushels of grain.

With this evidence of intensive corn-growing in Iron Age agriculture implied, it was immediately possible to interpret other features of the site. Large dug-out hollows would on modern ethnographic parallels be understood as working-places where the grain was husked and winnowed after the harvest; the burnt clay daub and stones were seen to belong to corn-drying furnaces in which, following a custom in wet countries that survived until the eighteenth century in the Scottish Highlands, the grain was parched to stop germination and prevent mould. The seed-corn was stored in granaries set on four stout posts above ground, out of reach of damp and rats; hay was dried on racks, in a manner still known to-day in, for instance, Norway and Switzerland, the post-holes of which survived in the Wiltshire site.

The household accommodated in the circular house could hardly have been more than that of a single family with dependants, and there is no evidence that more than one house existed in the farmyard at a time. Some pits may have served for water storage, but without natural sources of water on the spot cattle could hardly have been a very important feature of farming. The storage pits enable a reasoned estimate to be made of the land likely to have been farmed, assuming a yield of one-third of that obtainable in the district under modern conditions, and adding a proportion of seed-corn which, not being parched, would have been stored in granaries rather than in the underground pits. To provide an annual yield of something over seventy bushels, from five to seven acres of arable would have

sufficed, and it becomes apparent that a great number
of such farms could have flourished simultaneously on
the southern chalk and gravel lands where a suitably
light soil made clearance easy and agriculture with light-
traction ploughs a practicable matter.

The craft of weaving fabrics, although, as we have
seen, known from early in the Bronze Age in Britain,
seems in the Iron Age A culture to have been developed
along certain lines of specialization which necessitated
the use of distinctive types of bone combs for packing
the threads, and the spread of these particular techniques can thus be traced in the archæological record,
although the cloth itself has nowhere survived. Iron-
smelting and working does not seem to have been
carried out locally on the farms, and probably already
the blacksmith had emerged as an individual figure in
rural economy, the mysteries of his craft entitling him
to a certain supernatural status which is reflected in the
early Christian Irish prayers against the magic of
smiths, among other baleful persons. The Forest of Dean
iron ores probably formed the main sources of supply
in southern England at this time, those of the Sussex
Weald not being worked much before the first century
B.C. In Cornwall, tin, which had, of course, been exploited
since the Bronze Age, was being exported to the Greek
colony of Massilia by the third century B.C., and there
is evidence of Iron Age settlers in Cornwall, probably
before 100 B.C., and allied to the very late Hallstatt
culture of north Spain and west France, who may have
played a part in the trade, and would be culturally allied
to the Iron Age folk established elsewhere in southern
England. Soon after 100 B.C. a barbarous coinage of
bronze with a very high tin percentage was in use in

the areas of Iron Age A settlement, the type being derived from Central Gaulish coins, themselves copying the second-century bronze Massiliot coinage, and the use of tin in the British series again suggests Iron Age A contacts with the Cornish lodes. As we shall see, further continental contacts with Cornwall were to be established later in the Iron Age. A system of salt-making from sea-water, by pouring the brine over heated fire-bricks, was used by Iron Age A folk on the Lincolnshire and Dorset coasts, and was common in the Hallstatt culture of the Continent.

Certain hill-top defences in the chalk downs of Wessex seem to have been built even during the entrance phase of the Iron Age A culture (e.g. Figsbury, near Salisbury), though not apparently for anything more than occasional refuge during tribal wars. These hill-forts consist normally of a single bank and ditch ringing the hill-top and following the contours: the ditch is V-sectioned in the Late Bronze Age manner and the rampart often a simple heap of piled rubble sloped to the angle of rest—to use the nineteenth-century military terminology which is convenient in describing such fortifications; it is of 'glacis' construction, and designed to prolong the inner slope of the ditch so as to delay the rush of an attacking force. In some forts the larger blocks of chalk rubble may have been built up into a facing wall, or a dry-stone wall made in regions where suitable stone was obtainable, and it can sometimes be seen that the ramparts are on the line of an earlier palisade or fence set up in a bedding-trench.

Other hill-forts, however, known from excavation in Sussex (Hollingbury), Surrey (Wimbledon), Berkshire (Uffington Castle), Wiltshire (Yarnbury), and Dorset

(Maiden Castle), and therefore typical of the greater part of the Iron Age A province, have a more ambitious construction, in which a massive defence is built with a timber-work reinforcement, the uprights of which are set in two parallel rows bedded in the solid subsoil, and serve, with tie-beams, as the framework for a vertical-faced wall of rubble and soil, backed by a sloping ramp and separated from the ditch by a narrow platform or ' berm '. The amount of timber-work involved in such fortifications is of course considerable—in the small fort of Hollingbury in Sussex there must have been at least six hundred timbers, each six inches in diameter and up to eight feet or more in length, utilized in the primary upright construction alone, excluding transverse tie-beams or horizontal logs for facing. This type of construction is found in the continental homeland of the ancestors of the Iron Age A people, being known in Hallstatt forts in Germany, and we shall see its recurrence in later phases of the Iron Age in Britain. In Gaul the persistence of a similar technique into the first century B.C. was sufficiently marked for it to be named the Gallic Wall—*murus gallicus*—by Cæsar.

The most vulnerable point in a fortification is its entrance or gateway, and it is therefore not surprising that we find frequent indications of elaborate timber-work at these points in excavated hill-forts. Some entrances to Iron Age A forts are unelaborated, with evidence of a timber gate and nothing more, but a frequent constructional feature is the internal prolongation of timber-work, or combined timber- and earth-work, on both sides of the entrance so as to form a defended passage in which an enemy could be enfiladed from the adjoining ramparts. The actual gate, usually

double and closing on a central post, is set forward
of this passage-way in a line with the main rampart face;
and behind, and recessed into the inturned ends of the
ramparts, may be guard-chambers, one on each side of
the entrance. Evidence suggests that in some instances
at least a rampart-walk may have been carried over
the gateway on a timber bridge. The main long-distance
weapon against which such forts were built seems to
have been the spear (with a probable range of some
thirty yards), with swords for hand-to-hand fighting.
There is no direct evidence for the use of the bow and
arrow.

As we have seen, some Iron Age A forts were constructed soon after the arrival of their builders in Wessex,
and may have been designed against the older inhabitants of the region or for intertribal wars. But a
great number of such forts seem to have been constructed some generations after settlement was complete,
and after an interval of peace and agricultural prosperity.
There is often evidence of haste—forts were begun,
never to be completed, or defensive ditches dug (and
again not finished) round farmsteads (as at Little
Woodbury) or hamlet sites. Some of these unfinished
forts give us, incidentally, valuable information on the
method of construction of such defences: we can see in
one instance, at Ladle Hill in Hampshire, how the top
soil from the ditch was put on one side, so that the
rampart should be firmly based on the large blocks of
chalk rubble obtained in the deeper digging. In other
forts we can trace repairs and renovations—the gateway
in particular is sometimes remodelled and set in order
after a period of comparative disuse.

This all has a familiar ring to us to-day—southern

England hastily digging fortifications or improving old defences—and the parallel is indeed apt. In the middle of the third century B.C., when this sudden burst of fortification occurs, there was not only an invasion scare, but landings were taking place on the Sussex coast and elsewhere which strike a very martial note. To much of southern and south-western England it was never to be more than a scare, and the new elements brought by the invaders were slowly to spread and permeate the older traditions without the prelude of fire and sword, but in Sussex and in Kent we can see the appearance of a new people from across the Channel, carving out for themselves little kingdoms in Iron Age A territory.

The newcomers came indeed from much the same continental homeland as the first iron-users to reach England about 400 B.C., and in this invasion, which can be dated at about 250 B.C., we can see elements which link the Sussex and Kentish settlements to those of the Marne, and to the early phases of the culture of La Tène on the Continent. And at much the same time there appears in Yorkshire evidence of the invasions of a warrior aristocracy, of similar Marnian antecedents, establishing themselves among a population which consisted of various strains in which Late Bronze Age native stock and the late fifth-century Rhenish Iron Age immigrants must have fused to form a local version of the Hallstatt-derived cultures within the Iron Age A group. These new immigrant La Tène cultures from the Marne region, however, and others which we shall later trace in southern England, with some connexions in Brittany, are grouped together for convenience as the Iron Age B group of cultures of Britain.

L

In Sussex, the Marnian chieftains consolidated their
local conquests in the central block of downland, and
the hill-fort of Cissbury may have been their tribal
centre. From this region the spread of the Iron Age B
culture in various characteristic pottery styles can be
traced westwards and northwards, mixing with the
Iron Age A cultures and producing distinctive hybrid
forms in the field of pottery ornament, where the fine
curvilinear style of La Tène metal-work becomes transferred to pottery in a manner scarcely known on the
Continent. Much of this spread and intermixing takes
place long after the first invasions of 250 B.C.: the move
over the Sussex Weald into Kent seems to have taken
place by about 100 B.C., and a great deal of the beautiful
metal-work which is the main glory of Iron Age B was
made after this date in the south-west, though an earlier
school, dating from the late third or early second century, had produced consummate works of art in eastern
and north-eastern England.

It is in Yorkshire that the impact of the La Tène
war-bands is represented most dramatically in the
archæological record. We know from Ptolemy that
members of a Celtic tribe in Yorkshire shared with
others in France the name of the Parisii, and presumably
some members of this tribe migrated from the Seine to
the Yorkshire Wolds round about 250 B.C., though as
we shall see they do not seem to have been the main
ethnic component there. The Sussex and Kentish invasions apparently included women, for the pottery
traditions of the Marne are transferred across the
Channel in recognizable form; but in the East Riding
of Yorkshire the newcomers have more the appearance of
a small warrior caste, though including some women of

the ruling families—the pottery found in the Iron Age
B graves there is of native, not continental, ancestry,
and the intrusive elements are those of swords, shields,
horse-trappings and, above all, war-chariots, but there
are elaborate burials of women as well as of men. In
these vehicles of battle and parade at least a dozen
chieftains have been found buried, in cemeteries of up
to 500 graves where the commoners had to be contented
with a joint of pork as a viaticum.

The use of the two-wheeled horse-drawn chariot in
warfare seems to have been introduced into northern
Europe by the continental Celts at the beginning of the
La Tène phase, in the fifth century B.C., and chieftains
in the Middle Rhine and the Marne were buried with the
panoply of war in these vehicles, a large grave-pit being
dug to accommodate it. On the Continent, the changing
methods of warfare led to the chariot falling into disuse
by the second century B.C., but, after its introduction to
Britain in the mid-third century B.C. by the Iron Age B
folk of Marnian ancestry, it, and the tactics on the battle-
field which it implied, survived for a surprisingly long
time. As we shall see, chariot warfare on a large scale
was in force among the Belgic tribes in south-east
England in the middle of the first century B.C., and in
Lowland Scotland until the third century A.D. In northern
Ireland, where chariotry was introduced as a result of
the invasions of war-bands ultimately coming from
Yorkshire, a knowledge of the detailed appearance of
such vehicles was a living thing when the Ulster Cycle
of heroic legends was committed to writing in the eighth
or ninth centuries of the Christian era. From the archæological evidence of actual finds, supplemented by the
literary sources of Roman writers and the Irish sagas,

we can form a fair opinion of the appearance of the La
Tène chariot.

It was a very small, light structure, of sound car-
penters' and wheelwrights' craftsmanship. The wheels,
usually of twelve spokes, on turned wooden hubs with
iron nave-bands, were shod with tires of iron or even a
true steel wrought as a circle with a single join and
shrunk on to the wheel in the manner still traditional
to the English wheelwright, though unknown in the
ancient Mediterranean world, and a Celtic contribution
to coachbuilding practice. The wheel-base was about
4 feet 6 inches, still the standard gauge. The body was
little more than a platform less than four feet square
(' as long as a warrior's sword ', say the Irish tales),
with semicircular side-screens of wickerwork, but open
front and back—the Marnian chiefs lie at length in
their graves in the chariot, a position only possible
with an open front, and Cæsar's description of the
technique of British chariot warfare, with the warrior
stepping out on to the pole, again implies this. The
pole ran between the two horses that formed the normal
draught of the chariots—small ponies, between 11 and
13 hands—and these were harnessed by side-traces
attached to a swingletree at the rear, and a wooden
yoke on their necks, which bore decorative metal fair-
leads through which the reins ran. This use of the yoke
(common to all horse-drawn transport in the ancient
world) is an interesting survival of ox-traction ideas, and
the goad used by the charioteer in the Irish tales looks
like another similar inheritance. Small though the chariot
was, it bore both the warrior and his charioteer, the latter
doubtless crouching well forward over the swingletree.
The horses were provided with elaborate metal snaffle-bits.

To this description of the warrior's chariot, we may conveniently add a note on clothing. The continental Celts were a subject of comment among the Greeks and Romans for their trousers: a horseman's garment which, like so much in their art, seems to have come from the Orient, and worn, it seems, tight at the ankle. A love of bright colours, and the use of stripes and check patterns that might be ancestral to the tartan series, are attested, but in battle at least the rank and file fought naked save for the distinctive metal collar or torc.

To the Yorkshire Parisii may be attributed much of the fine decorated metal-work of the early school of Celtic art in Britain, finding expression in a subtle treatment of balanced though not obviously symmetrical curves based ultimately on classical tendril patterns, either treated in relief or in delicate engraving on the bronze mountings of sword-scabbards, the typical La Tène oblong shield, or other articles of ceremonial parade for warrior or horses. Among the Yorkshire aristocratic graves is at least one of a woman, buried with an iron, bronze-mounted mirror, and her status reminds us of the Amazonian queens of Celtic Britain known in later centuries, Boudicca of the Iceni and Cartimandua of the Brigantes: Tacitus expressly states that the Celtic tribes in Britain made no distinction of sex in their rulers. Finely decorated metal mirrors become, by the first century B.C., one of the most beautiful types of Iron Age B metal-work in Britain. The resemblances between the Parisian 'tendril' style and that of a group of Hungarian swords might be explicable in terms of the Central European physical type represented in the Yorkshire graves.

By the incidence of finds of such metal-work of the

early school, together with collateral archæological evidence and that of philology and the early native literary sources, it is possible to trace a movement of people whose immediate ancestry lay in the Yorkshire Marnians into west Yorkshire (probably to the mouth of the Ribble) and thence by sea to south-western Scotland and Ulster. Here the exploits of the warrior aristocracy of overlords, their wealth based on herds of cattle rather than on extensive corn-growing, and their warfare conducted from the chariot, were handed down in oral tradition until the scribes of the early Christian Church wrote down these tales of a remote Iron Age past. It is difficult to date the arrival of the descendants of the Parisii in Ulster, but a date around 150 B.C. seems probable.

In south-west England, as we have seen, the tin of Cornwall had already found continental purchasers in the Massiliot Greek traders in the third century: we know also that the trade route was by sea from St. Michael's Mount to the mouth of the Loire, thence overland by a thirty days' journey to the Gulf of Lions (a route which originally had come into use to avoid the Carthaginian blockade of the Straits of Gibraltar). It is therefore not surprising that we should find evidence of contact between southern Brittany and Cornwall by about 100 B.C.—cliff-castles defended by multiple stone and rubble ramparts drawn across the necks of promontories in Cornwall (as on Gurnard's Head) reflect a type of fortification in the Morbihan which was the outcome of warfare using the sling rather than the spear as the weapon of attack, and to these innovations in armament we will shortly return. But the cliff-castles are not the only evidence for Breton contacts with the south-west, for distinctive pottery types related to the same region can be traced not only in the tin-producing areas but, significantly enough, up the coasts of the Severn towards the easily accessible iron ores of the Forest of Dean. Metal-prospecting, then, seems to lie behind what may be yet another element in the Iron Age B complex of cultures of La Tène derivation in England, for some settlement undoubtedly must have taken place up to the skirts of the Cotswolds, otherwise an Iron Age A province.

The Forest of Dean iron-workings must be the explanation of the remarkable form of currency that was in circulation within the south-western Iron Age B province in the first century B.C.—the use of flat iron bars, their shape perhaps based on the rough-outs ('moods') of swords, in a system of graduated weights. These currency-bars were commented on by Cæsar in the middle of the first century B.C. as one of the three forms of currency then in circulation in southern England, the other two being the cast coins of bronze with a high tin content already seen as apparently an Iron Age A invention, and the struck coins of gold which as we shall see later were first minted by the Belgæ about the time of his invasions.

In Worcestershire, on Bredon Hill, a hill-fort was built by immigrant metal-traders about 50 B.C., with a simple 'glacis' construction rampart, to be refortified nearly a century later in a manner which suggests the recrudescence of local Iron Age A traditions, with a long inturned entrance in timber and stone-work, a probable bridge to carry the rampart-walk over, and a great double gate which in a final attack on the fortress had been brought crashing and burning to the ground, crushing some of the members of the attacking force and bringing with it what on the evidence of excavation can only be interpreted as a row of human heads that had once graced its top. We know something of the streak of savagery in the Celts that had one outcome in head-hunting from the evidence of sculpture and sanctuaries adorned with actual human skulls in the south of France, and the final massacre at the Bredon gateway brings home forcibly the grim barbarism of these forts on our British hill-tops.

Save for the gradual infiltration of Marnian and other Iron Age B elements, the Wessex downs had remained in the possession of the descendants of the Iron Age A colonists from the fourth century B.C. until the middle of the first. The invasion scare of the years around 250 B.C. was over, and we can presume a state of prosperous agriculture punctuated by intertribal warfare of a sort for many generations, and then suddenly the archæological evidence shows a tremendous building of new hill-forts and a reconstruction of old defences in a novel and impressive manner, while certain modifications and innovations in pottery types imply a new element in the population.

To seek the origins of this we must turn to the Continent and to recorded history. It will be remembered that, largely as a result of the Cornish tin trade, relations between south-west England and Brittany had been established, probably as early as the third, certainly by the end of the second century B.C. The Celtic tribe of the Veneti, occupying the area now Brittany, had at least one recognized trading-mart in Britain recorded by Strabo, and the archæological evidence, as we have seen, confirms this trade relationship. In 56 B.C. Julius Cæsar carried out his well-known attack on the Veneti, involving a desperate sea-fight against the great Venetic shallow-draught ships, with their leather sails and iron anchor-chains, that are described so vividly in the *Commentaries* as the writer stresses the difficulty of the enterprise. The conquered Veneti were used as a grim warning to the Celts that Roman ambassadors could not be put in chains with impunity: apart from the decimation of the Venetic fleet and army, all who could be captured were carried off as slaves. Before the Roman attack the Veneti had turned to Britain for aid; now it is surely not improbable that such fugitive chiefs and warriors as could escape in the remnants of the fleet may have sailed across the Channel to the Dorset coast.

Such seems the probable historical setting of the sudden appearance in Wessex of novel techniques of fortification alien to the old Hallstatt tradition based on the thrown spear, but related to another and more effective long-range weapon, the sling. The Veneti were famed among the Gauls as slingers, and in the cliff-castles of southern Brittany sling-stones are abundant. And the multiplication of ramparts, seen here, in the Cornish promontory forts, and above all in the great hill-forts of Wessex of this time, was the answer to this particular weapon—the increasing of the distance between the attackers and the defenders of the fort in the face of a weapon with a range of up to at least one hundred yards, over three times that of the spear.

The enormous hill-fort of Maiden Castle in Dorset took on its present form of tremendous strength and complexity under this intrusive Venetic element in Wessex: it may well have been the major stronghold of the invaders, adapted and enlarged from the earlier Iron Age A defences. The new work revealed by excavation here, and comparable in general external appearance to that of many Wessex hill-forts, took the form of multiple ramparts and ditches, the ramparts being built in a modified 'glacis' technique with the addition of massive stone walling at the rear. The gateways were elaborated with a maze of flanking horn-works, and forward of the main ramparts by the gate were found built platforms to offer vantage-points for the slingers, whose ammunition was found stored in huge quantities in pits behind the defences—one such sling-stone dump comprised over 22,000 selected beach pebbles.

Other forts in the south-west show the characteristic multiple rampart construction which seems, as we have seen, to be of Venetic origin, and the intrusion of the refugee remnants of the fighting forces of this tribe with their new armaments and tactics must have ushered in a time of troubles reflected in this refortification of tribal strongholds. There is some Breton influence perceptible on the pottery styles associated with the occupation of such sites, and other modifications look like the copying of metal bowls in clay—the historical setting makes it improbable that many Venetic-women could have escaped slavery and come to England, and local pottery evolution with some influence from imported metal-work brought in by the warriors seems probable. An iron anchor and chain found in a coastal hill-fort at Belbury in Dorset offers striking confirmation of Cæsar's statement with regard to the Venetic ships referred to above.

By the middle of the first century B.C., then, there was in southern England a mixed collection of tribes within the archæological group of Iron Age B, having in common ancestral traditions linking them to the La Tène cultures of Europe. In about 75, and again about 50 B.C., there were further immigrations to southern and eastern England from the north Gaulish regions belonging to the Belgic tribes, and these Belgæ (Iron Age C) will be discussed towards the end of this chapter. For the present, however, we must continue the tale of the mixed traditions of the Iron Age A and B cultures in the south-west, and consider their interrelation with those in Yorkshire, while ultimately turning to the Highland Zone of Britain to consider the derivation of the early iron-using cultures in Scotland and in Ireland.

The south-west and the north-east Iron Age B provinces, though distant one from another, were nevertheless linked by the natural route afforded by the line of the Jurassic rocks, which stretch north-eastwards from the Mendips and Cotswolds across the southern Midlands to Lincolnshire. Along this belt of high, relatively lightly wooded country, avoiding alike the heavy damp oak forests and the swampy river valleys, a movement of trade and population had been relatively continuous since neolithic times (when indeed the main pattern of human distribution and movement in Britain had been formed, to last into early historic times). But perhaps at no period is the contact between north-east and south-west so clear as during the first couple of centuries B.C., and particularly so in the interactions of the schools of Iron Age B metal-work.

The early school of metal-work, with designs based on tendril-*motifs* and which we may assign to the Yorkshire culture of the Parisii, dates as we have seen from the second half of the third century and probably continues well into the second: with it can be associated a characteristic type of iron or bronze snaffle-bit which on the Continent is distinctively Marnian. This type of bit is, however, also characteristic of the south-western province, as are other elements of chariot-mountings and horse-harness, and the intermediate examples known are strung along the Jurassic Belt; and though the south-western material is on the present evidence almost entirely within the first century B.C., contacts must have been established earlier than this. Some continuity between the two areas in matters of horsemanship and coachbuilding lie behind the interchange of ideas in decorative art which we can now trace, with sites intermediate between Yorkshire and Somerset (such as Hunsbury near Northampton) producing just the combination of styles that might be expected. The use of a hatched background in a 'matting' technique to emphasize the curvilinear patterns incised on metal seems characteristic of the Somerset school, and in Yorkshire such hatching is used in combination with derivatives of the older tendril *motifs* to form a pattern in itself. The construction and decoration of bronze sword-scabbards again show two related but distinctive schools of armourers, the eastern group having probably closer and earlier continental parallels than those of the west.

The transference of metal-work designs to pottery in the southern provinces of Iron Age B has already been commented upon, and one of the sites in which this style is particularly well developed is in itself one of the most interesting and most adequately excavated settlements of the south-western group, in which Iron Age A elements can be traced although the B culture predominates. In the marshland near Glastonbury in Somerset at least two villages were established in the first century B.C., perhaps one of them a little earlier, and the natural difficulties of the terrain were overcome by ingenious and extensive timber-work construction. It seems scarcely probable that permanent settlements would be made in a region half swamp, half actual lake, unless some stress of political conditions led communities to take refuge in these dreary marshes, the haunt of pelican and cormorant, heron, bittern, wild duck, swan, and crane, but unless the Venetic invasion after 56 B.C. be claimed as contributory, the reason is still to seek.

The site was in a fresh-water marsh with a thick growth of willow, alder, and hazel, among which in the pools grew bog-bean, water-lilies, spear-wort, and pond-weeds. The undergrowth was cut down, and on the swampy peat a great foundation of timber and brushwood was laid down to cover a roughly triangular area: logs, chiefly of alder, but also including oak and ash and birch evidently felled on drier ground and brought to the site, were laid in two layers at right angles and covered thickly with brushwood. Clay, stones, and rubble were also used. Wooden piles were driven in to steady the mass, and the whole area was surrounded by a close-set palisade of posts, up to four abreast, cut to a point with axes and bill-hooks, and driven down into the peat. At one side was a causeway built of stone with timber reinforcement, and a landing-stage which must have been made in a stretch of relatively open water along which dug-out canoes could come.

Upon the substructure of timber and brushwood, floors of clay were laid as the foundations of circular houses, of which at least seventy existed, though not necessarily all in occupation at the same time, with

diameters ranging from 18 to 28 feet. The structure of
the house was on a framework of closely set poles up to
nine inches in diameter, and the absence of any central
setting of timbers implies that these poles were bent
over to form a domed roof and wall in one. There had
been rectangular buildings on or near the site, for re-
used mortised beams were found in the substructure,
suggesting buildings of the type of the Late Bronze Age
house in Ireland at Balinderry mentioned in Chapter IV.
The circular houses were frequently repaired and the
wall-circle of poles renewed, while the gradual sinking
of the site necessitated the constant renewal of the clay
floors and central hearths, in one instance ten times
during the life of the village, and frequently three or
four times. Certain square settings of posts suggest
granaries of the type already referred to in connexion
with Iron Age A farms, but no direct evidence of corn
storage was met with. If the villagers were themselves
farmers, their fields must have been beyond the swamps
on higher ground. Grain was certainly used by the inhabitants of the village, both wheat and barley being
found, the former in some curious whole-meal cakes
apparently made with honey, and flour was ground not
only on the old-fashioned saddle-shaped grinding stone
but with the rotary quern, not it seems in use in England
until the middle of the first century B.C. A dwarf form
of broad bean was also cultivated for food, and domesticated animals included the horse, ox, sheep, goat, pig,
and dog.

The preservation of wood in the waterlogged peat
enables us to see much of the work of the carpenter
which has elsewhere perished—tool-handles, a ladder,
a chopping-block, a solid wooden door 3 feet 6 inches

high and 18 inches wide, troughs, tubs, and bowls turned on a pole lathe, some with fine incised ornament in the metal-work style, and, also turned, axle-boxes and spokes for wheels. These may have belonged to chariots or to carts, for which horses were harnessed sometimes with the metal snaffle-bit of Marnian type, but more often with the older type of Hallstatt origin with bone or horn cheek-pieces, known in England since the Late Bronze Age. The iron tools found are, as might be expected, mainly those of the carpenter and woodman—bill-hooks, adzes, gouges, files, saws, and sickles—and spears or swords or daggers are very scarce, though there are some sling-stones (perhaps for hunting). Iron currency bars relate the villagers to the Iron Age B monetary system, and the gambling instinct of the Celt is shown by the dice-boxes and dice of a distinctive type.

While spinning and weaving was doubtless a craft carried on in every household, there is nevertheless a suggestion that one and perhaps two other houses were those of weavers (using weaving-combs of Iron Age A type, though common in B sites) who were producing more cloth than was needed by their own families. Bronze-smiths too had at various times worked in different houses at the edge of the village (probably to minimize the risk of fire). Objects of lead and tin imply trade contacts with the Mendips and Cornwall, and shale for bracelets probably comes from the Dorset coast, where it had been exploited by Iron Age A people. A curious technique of making textile braids suitable for girths and reins, and known as tablet weaving, is known to have been carried out by the Iron Age B folk in the south-west, at one of the Glastonbury marsh-villages and elsewhere.

From this remarkably detailed picture of an Iron Age
B settlement in south-west England, we must turn to
north Britain and consider the sequence of affairs there
following on the arrival and consolidation of the Hallstatt and La Tène elements in the south. As we saw in
Chapter IV, there continued in many regions of the
Highland Zone a tardy Late Bronze Age, in the main
derived from the traditions of the Middle Bronze Age,
and although little affected, if at all, by the intrusive
Late Bronze Age cultures of the south, it nevertheless
developed an important series of bronze weapon types
which were able to compete in the European markets.
The probable immigrants implied by the ' flat-rimmed '
pottery would also have contributed to the population.
But with the coming of iron as a cheap metal, the
bronze-smiths of the British Highland Zone were faced
with a steadily diminishing demand for their output,
and we have seen the pathetic case of the Irish bronze-
smith who set up his shop in the remote Shetlands
after all local markets had been closed to his products.

We have seen that there was a move in the second
century B.C. from the territory of the Parisii in Yorkshire to southern Scotland and to Ulster, and no doubt
some of the chieftains and camp-followers settled in the
Lowlands, but the first distinctively Iron Age culture
we can detect in Scotland does not seem likely, on the
available evidence, to date much before 100 B.C. This
culture is mainly represented by a series of hill-forts
whose constructional feature, typified by one near
Abernethy, is essentially that of timber and stonework
which we have seen is of Hallstatt ancestry, and which
is represented in the Iron Age A forts of southern
England by modified forms where earth and rubble are

used instead of the unobtainable stone. In the Scottish examples the result of accidental or deliberate ignition of the timber-work during attack has often led to the stonework being slagged or 'vitrified' into solid masses (and this too is often seen in comparable French forts within the first couple of centuries B.C.), and such forts are grouped along the west coast from the Firth of Lorne to the Solway, up the Great Glen, and around the Moray Firth and the Tay estuary.

The material culture of the chieftains who built these numerous tribal strongholds has many features which relate it to the A rather than to the B group of Iron Age cultures (brooches of early La Tène type, characteristic of south English Iron Age A sites, ring-headed pins, and bone bridle cheek-pieces, for instance), and although the Scottish distribution is usually interpreted as representing an east-coast invasion from the Continent, it seems more explicable as a westerly landing of English origin. It is difficult to account for refugee chieftains of Iron Age A heritage without some political disturbance in southern England, but the Marnian invasions of the mid-third century B.C. might well provide such a context. Movement out of the Wessex region northwards would not be along the Jurassic ridge if knowledge of the Yorkshire landings had reached the south, and up the Welsh Marches and into Cheshire a chain of hill-forts show in their construction Iron Age A techniques including the timber-and-stone *murus gallicus*, implying a strong tradition established along this route. At least one fort (Old Oswestry) is known to belong to a relatively early phase of Iron Age A. From the North Welsh or Cheshire coasts, to which progress might well have been spread over a century or more,

M

exploratory parties could have taken sail to land in Galloway and the Clyde mouth at the end of the second century B.C., or indeed earlier.

A second culture within the Scottish Iron Age whose monuments are again strongly defended, but of the nature of clan or family centres, is represented by the famous structures known as brochs, over five hundred of which are known from Skye and the Outer Hebrides northwards to Caithness, Orkney, and Shetland. Typically, the brochs are circular structures of dry walling, with a single entrance often with a guard-chamber in the thickness of the wall, and galleries and stairways constructed in like manner between the outer and inner wall faces. The internal diameter may be between 25 and 35 feet, the walls up to 15 feet thick and in some brochs at least rising to a height of 40 feet or more, though the majority must have been lower, perhaps averaging 15 or 20 feet. These remarkable buildings are obviously designed for defence—particularly in Shetland and Orkney outer defences of walls or ditches are added, in a manner comparable to the bailey of a Norman motte-and-bailey castle, and in the enclosed area are smaller buildings—and equally obviously they belong to a tradition based on the circular-house plan. In themselves a phenomenon unique to Scotland, they must represent a peculiar and individual adaptation, for defensive purposes, of the same architectural conception as the timber-built circular houses of the southern English Iron Age A and B complexes, and as we shall see, North British timber structures similarly related are known to exist.

The material culture represented in the brochs re-inforces the connexions with the south implicit in their plans. All the equipment of the specialized weaving industry of the mixed A-B culture as seen for instance in the villages in the Glastonbury marshes is represented in the brochs—the typical weaving-combs, bone bobbins, and so on—and common to the two cultures also are the oblong dice of Glastonbury type. The broch pottery suggests Iron Age A strains in the population, though one or two pieces with incised animals suggest the Iron Age B, or La Tène, art-style, and other objects such as bone spear-points and triangular metal crucibles again relate the two widely separated regions of south-west England and northern Scotland, and even the masonry and circular plan of the brochs recall the ring-forts of Cornwall (such as Chun Castle) associated with the Breton metal-prospectors in that region. Allied to the broch culture is that known from a group of circular aisled houses ('wheel-houses') in the Hebrides and in Orkney and Shetland, one at least of which has produced pottery of Iron Age B affinities.

The evidence for dating the broch culture in Scotland is slight, but fairly conclusive for placing it as a whole before the first century A.D. In England, as we have seen, trade relationships had been established at least by 100 B.C. between Brittany and the south-west, to be followed by an invasion of dispossessed Venetic chieftains in 56 B.C., and by this time also some pressure on the south-west was probably being exercised by the Belgic tribes established in the Thames estuary by 75 B.C. Conditions were therefore such as to render likely an emigration of some of the mixed A-B Iron Age population from the regions now Somerset, Devon, and Cornwall. In Derbyshire, in west Yorkshire around Settle, and again in Northumberland, characteristic

Iron Age B weaving equipment shows that colonization of the region from south-west England took place, at the end of the first century B.C. or later. There may have been landings in Ireland—the tribal name of the Dumnonii is attested here by native literary evidence as well as in the Devonshire area (and the Damnonii in south-west Scotland may be related). There is a die of Glastonbury type from County Waterford and weaving-combs from County Dublin and Loughcrew, and finds in Galloway identical to those of west Yorkshire are dated in the first century A.D. In the Clyde and Solway coastal areas the primary settlements of the builders of the *murus gallicus* forts of the Abernethy type should already have been established and so have deterred fresh colonists, but beyond the Firth of Lorne the coast may have been, literally, almost clear of rivals, unless some of the 'duns', at present undated, should prove to be of pre-broch date.

The brochs are sited with clear relation to good farming land. Extensive sheep-breeding must lie behind the abundant weaving equipment, and there is indirect evidence of the export of wool by broch inhabitants in Roman times; but the defensive character of so many brochs implies anything but settled conditions, and rather gives a picture of raiding and reiving and of clan feuds. It seems that the southern ancestry of the broch people served to keep the Roman Empire before their minds even in their northern isolation, for the chieftains of the Orkneys appear to have made formal submission to Claudius after his conquest of southern Britain in the years following A.D. 43, in accordance with the not uncommon custom of tribes in Gaul or southern England who saw the advantage to be gained from a politic alliance with the superior power of Rome.

We may with reason therefore regard northern Scotland by the end of the first century B.C. as constituting
two major provinces, both ancestrally linked to southern
English Iron Age communities—the Abernethy people,
of Iron Age A traditions, occupying the territory between
the Forth-Clyde line on the south to the Great Glen
and the Moray Firth on the north, and north and west
of this province that of the broch folk, with probably
a mixed A and B cultural tradition, in which, however,
the B element seems predominant. The older (Late
Bronze Age) population, including the makers of 'flat-
rimmed' pottery, must not of course be forgotten. In
Lowland Scotland the Abernethy people seem to have
had at least coastal settlements from the Solway to the
Clyde, but for the Iron Age over the greater part of
the area no field monuments immediately recognizable
as distinctive of a localized culture, in the way that
a broch or a *murus gallicus* fort is identifiable, have been
traced, though hill-forts are common in south-east Scotland. There are significant hints relating the south-west
region to both Ulster and the Isle of Man.

We have seen that a movement of chieftains and followers took place from Yorkshire to northern Ireland
probably about 150 B.C.—the overlords who established
themselves as a dominant aristocracy in Ulster and whose
traditions were handed down into the Middle Ages.
Finds of metal-work of fine quality show that settlements
were also made in south-west Scotland at the time of
the original, second-century migration, and derivatives
show that the traditions were sufficiently firmly established for the craft of the metal-worker to develop along
individual lines. An essential feature of warfare as
conducted by the warrior-aristocrats in both Yorkshire

and Ulster in the second century was the use of the two-wheeled chariot, of Marnian or Middle Rhenish origin; and the survival of chariot warfare in southern and eastern Scotland until the Roman campaigns in the time of Agricola again implies a strongly implanted tradition in that region having its roots in the culture of the Yorkshire Parisii. Surviving sword-scabbards tell the same tale of a common armament in the three regions, and the vanquished Caledonians depicted on the locally carved distance-slabs on the Antonine Wall hold the typical oblong La Tène type of shield, again known from Yorkshire and inferentially from the Irish literary evidence. The cumulative evidence therefore suggests that south of the area occupied by the builders of the Abernethy forts and their descendants there was, at the beginning of the Christian era, a province whose cultural roots were partly in the Yorkshire 'Parisian' culture of the third and second centuries B.C. In south-east Scotland, hill-forts originally consisting of a single massive stone wall seem to have been remodelled with additional defensive works consisting of multiple ditches and stone-faced rubble ramparts, very much in the manner of the refortification of south-west English hill-forts already described, and their occurrence may indicate the arrival in the region of dispossessed chieftains with Iron Age B or even 'Venetic' traditions.

In certain regions in south-west Scotland artificial timber constructions situated in marshes or lakes have been found (for instance at Buston or Lochlee in Ayrshire), and all come within the generic term of 'crannogs', used particularly of similar structures in Ireland. The Irish crannogs at least may have Late Bronze Age origins (as at Ballinderry, already referred to in Chapter

IV), but the majority known seem to date from early
medieval times, while in Scotland several date from the
first two centuries of the Christian era, though others are
medieval or even later. In the earliest Scottish crannogs
(first century A.D.) the structure seems to have been a
circular house built on a platform of timber and brushwood in the Glastonbury manner, but a sufficiently
obvious and common technique to have little or no cultural significance. But the type of house represented in
these Scottish sites, with a central hearth and timber-
framed walls, can be better understood with reference
to recent discoveries in the Isle of Man.

Here the skilled and total excavation of three sites
(which, with their successive rebuildings, gives us in all
the details of nine houses of similar type) has revealed
a consistent form of farmstead of circular plan and remarkably interesting internal structure dating from the
first couple of centuries A.D. The total overall diameter
ranged from 70 to 90 feet, and the sites were each surrounded by a shallow ditch and a bank of earth piled
up against the outer wall of close-set oak posts. The
excavator has claimed that the entire area within this
wall was covered over by a low-pitched roof of turf
and sods carried on rafters which were supported by
concentric rings of widely spaced posts, the roof rising
to a maximum height of about 12 feet. A secondary
circular wall within the structure, enclosing an area
about 35 feet across in the largest house, defined what
was clearly the family living-room, with a plank or log
floor and a central hearth. To its entrance there ran a
paved pathway from a corresponding opening in the
outer wall and bank, but the remainder of the roofed
area between the two circular walls was unpaved, or

with patches of paving only, and could be interpreted as accommodation for cattle and perhaps retainers of the chieftain who lived in greater comfort within the inner dwelling-room. The occupational debris implied a little metal-working, some spinning and weaving, and from the preponderance of cattle bones among the food refuse and the location of the sites in relation to natural pasturage, the agricultural economy behind the farmsteads seems distinctively that of stock-breeders rather than that of large-scale growers of corn, though grain was used and ground in the settlements.

In the light of this detailed Manx evidence we can see that basically similar houses existed among the south-western Scottish crannog series in Dumbartonshire and Ayrshire and probably elsewhere, and comparable structures seem likely to be represented in Ireland by many, and probably most, of the circular earthworks about 100 feet in diameter known as 'raths': one at Lissue near Belfast certainly contained such a house dating from the eighth or ninth century A.D., and the type is presumably some centuries earlier in origin. It is probably represented by a few unexcavated examples in southern Scotland, for instance near Hawick. The Irish legends of the Ulster Cycle, that contain so much material relating to the Yorkshire-derived Iron Age culture of the second century B.C., depict the chariot-using chieftains as living in large houses whose plan and structure, as it appears in the texts, can be best interpreted from the Manx or Scottish circular buildings just described. It seems probable therefore that the origin of this interesting roofed farmstead (for such it seems to have been) may lie within the Iron Age B complex and be allied to the Yorkshire culture of the Parisii, or at least may be a development in the derivative areas of this culture where the climate was notable for frequent and heavy rain.

A curious class of structure, common to Scotland and Ireland, but also known in Cornwall and west France, is a narrow underground chamber roofed with stone slabs carried on side walling. In Ireland such souterrains may go back to the local Late Bronze Age, in Cornwall they are not likely to be earlier than the first century B.C.; one in Shetland is earlier than a broch, and those in Lowland Scotland are second century A.D. Some might be refuges, but on the whole cellars for food storage seems the more likely explanation for these curious structures, and, if they can be considered as culturally linked, some connexion with the south-western Iron Age B culture seems probable. A restricted group of such structures in Jutland seems explicable as the result of Irish or Scottish contacts in the late pre-Roman Iron Age of Denmark, and it is probable that some influence of the long, rectangular Iron Age house of Jutland and adjacent regions can be traced on Scottish buildings apparently approximately contemporary with brochs in Caithness and elsewhere.

It should be mentioned here that there may be a large number of fortified sites in Ireland and Scotland as yet unrecognized as of Iron Age date. In North Wales large hill-forts such as Tre'r Ceiri were built and occupied well into the period of the Roman occupation, perhaps as part of an Imperial frontier policy of utilizing native forms of defence against the Irish raiders, and many of the large fortifications of other regions within the Highland Zone may be Roman or later in date, but in the direct line of Iron Age tradition, such as the fine stone-built fort of Carlwárla in Derbyshire. In Ireland, excavated forts of various types have been found to fall within the first ten centuries A.D., but many characteristic types (as for instance the promontory forts or cliff-castles of south-east Ireland) are as yet undated. In Scotland there are an enormous number of forts and 'duns', especially in the West Highland areas, and while some of these may even be medieval, others may well date to the pre-Roman Iron Age. In such regions as west and north Scotland, Iron Age types of building certainly survived well into the Dark Ages and beyond, and the Norse raiders must have had their forts, such as those which have been identified in the Isle of Man. Recent field-work has shown that the apparent concentration of 'small forts' in the region between Hadrian's and the Antonine Wall is more complex than at first appeared, and the sites included in the estimate may range over a period from the Iron Age to medieval times.

But while these localized developments out of the old Hallstatt and La Tène cultures were growing up in the comparative isolation of North Britain, further invasions had been taking place into southern and south-eastern England which represented a third strain in the European-derived Iron Age cultures of that region. The cultures grouped in England as those of Iron Age C have already been referred to, in connexion with the Venetic invasion in 56 B.C., for both the two main invasive or colonizing movements that can be recognized took place in the first century B.C.—the first round about 75 B.C., the second in about 50 B.C. The historical sources (basically, the writings of Julius Cæsar) enable us to date these invasions with some degree of accuracy, in the same way as was possible with that of the dispossessed Veneti, and in like manner we can give a name to the invaders—the confederacy of tribes of North Gaul known as the Belgæ.

Since the eighth century B.C. there had been intermittent pressure on the Celtic tribes of the Rhineland from the Teutonic peoples to the north and east beyond the Elbe—peoples who included the tribes of the Cimbri and the Germani—and indeed by the sixth century considerable Teutonic elements had spread as far south as Cologne and the Moselle, and something of a political boundary appears to have been established early in La Tène times. But by the beginning of the first century B.C. there had grown up in what is now north France and Belgium a mixed Celtic and Teutonic people, embracing half a dozen tribes in a more or less unified Belgic confederacy, and Cæsar explicitly states that contingents of these Belgæ had crossed over to south-east Britain, primarily for plunder and warfare, but remaining to be in occupation there by the time of his first arrival in 55 B.C. Now the evidence of archæology and history concur in placing this first Belgic invasion within fairly narrow limits at about 75 B.C., and it is from this date that prehistory and history overlap in England, and we can interpret the archæological evidence in terms of individuals known by name, their dynasties and their seats of government.

Among the tribes included in the Belgic confederacy of the Continent were the Catuvellauni, settled in the Marne region, and we find a new tribe bearing this ancestral name in possession of a large part of south-eastern England by 55 B.C. The Catuvellauni (whose name probably means 'The Mighty Warriors') seem to have been the dominant element in the war-bands

who had set off from Gaul, and, as the evidence of
archæology shows, came into the Thames estuary and
penetrated into the hinterland by means of the rivers—
into Kent by way of the Stour and Medway, by various
streams into Essex, by the Thames itself, and up the
valley of the Lea in Hertfordshire—suggesting the
Teutonic strain in their composition in this adroit
exploitation of the waterways among the forests. And
near the Lea, at Wheathamstead, was built a Belgic
town, with an area of over 100 acres defended by the
natural forests and valleys, helped by prodigious artificial ditches; and here, as chieftain of the Catuvellauni,
ruled Cassivellaunus, 'the first British personality, the
first man in England whose name we know'.

It is not our place here to enter into the history of
the Belgic princes, or of Cæsar's campaigns, but already
by 55 B.C. Kent, Middlesex, and Hertfordshire were
under Belgic dominion, and later Essex, the territory of
the Iron Age A tribe of the Trinobantes, was added;
and under Tasciovanus, ruling from Verulamium (St.
Albans, whence the seat of power seems to have moved
after Cæsar's sack of the Wheathamstead oppidum), and
his son Cunobelinus, with his capital in the recently
acquired Trinobantian territory at Camulodunum
(Colchester), the Belgic dominion of the Catuvellaunian
dynasty was extended north to Cambridge and north-
westwards to include Northamptonshire by the third
decade of the first century A.D.

Although it had a start of twenty-five years, the
Catuvellaunian hegemony in south-eastern England was
not unchallenged. In the Belgic homeland after the
conquest of Gaul there had been a rebellion, and the re-
calcitrant leader of the tribe of the Atrebates, Commius,

fled to England in about 50 B.C. With his court
and followers he seems to have landed, perhaps in
Sussex, and set up a new kingdom for himself. Under
his sons a capital was founded on the site of Calleva
Atrebatum (Silchester), where Epillus, one of these sons,
minted a coinage which included inscriptions in Roman
letters, recording names of rulers or of mints, and similar
coins were struck by the Catuvellaunian princes and
imitated in the non-Belgic regions on the outskirts of
the ruling tribes. Such coins, derived from fourth-
century gold staters of Philip of Macedon which had
come into circulation in the Roman provinces as a result
of loot and tribute-money collected after the wars in
the east in the early second century, had been minted in
Gaul for some time, and the British series are especially
valuable for working out the tribal history and dynastic
relationships of the Belgæ. The use of Roman letters
and the title *rex* (used by Cunobelin) give an interesting
light on the literacy of the Belgic aristocrats—they must
many of them have been bilingual—and the use of a
modified D to represent a specifically Celtic consonantal
sound in such names as Aððedomaros and Anteðrig on
coins shows that conscious efforts to relate phonetics and
script were being made among Celtic-speaking people
in Britain.

The House of Commius eventually ruled territory
which certainly included Hampshire and Berkshire, and
probably part at least of Wiltshire—a Kentish province
ruled by Epillus had been lost to Cunobelin some time
before A.D. 40, but the Sussex tribe of the Regni formed
also a part of the Commian kingdom. The sons of
Commius had no love for the east Belgic power centred
on Cunobelin, and therefore turned to Rome—one son

had fled as a suppliant to Augustus, and another appealed
to Claudius, and when Roman power was becoming
a reality in England, the Regni under Cogidumnus,
successor to a son of Commius, were quick to side with
the invader against the hated Catuvellaunian dynasty.
There had been earlier moves westward of anti-
Cunobelin elements, emigrants from Kent after the
fall of Dubnovellaunus there.

The Iron Age C cultures which represent the rule of
the Catuvellaunian and the Commian dynasties in the
archæological record show, as might be expected, an
increasing contact with Rome. Pottery types relate both
groups to their continental homeland, but though there
is no doubt that the first Belgic invasion of 75 B.C. was
accompanied, or very closely followed, by a considerable
contingent of farmers, artisans, and other peaceable
settlers, the composition of the entourage of Commius
is not so clear. A refugee chieftain is not likely to bring
potters with him, but the appearance of certain types
of wheel-made pottery for the first time in southern
England seems likely to be associated at least with
immigrants subsequent to the establishment of Commian rule in southern England. The exploitation of the
valleys and the heavier clay-lands for agriculture seems
to be accompanied by the use of a heavier plough with
a massive coulter, probably ploughing a strip-field
which may share a Teutonic ancestry with the similar
forms of the Middle Ages. Relatively little is known in
detail of the Belgic settlements, but the townships seem
to have straggled without much defined ground-plan,
and the houses so far recovered are unimpressive wooden
structures. Much use was made of lines of earthwork or
dykes for defences, utilizing also the areas of woodland

and marsh for natural defence. Tribal centres moved down from the hill-tops to the lower land—that of the Regni was indeed named Noviomagos, the new site on the plain.

Some remarkable burial-vaults are, however, known, which throw a vivid light on the beliefs of the Celts about the other world and, by implication, their customs in this. We know from classical writers that their ideas included that of a naïve, material immortality in which one could even repay debts contracted on earth, and in the rich Chieftains' Graves of early La Tène times in the Rhineland (second half of the fifth century B.C.) we find equipment for a party for two beyond the grave —wine in imported Etruscan jars, Greek cups to drink it from. In certain Belgic tombs in Catuvellaunian terri- tory this cheering hospitality of the Celt is again seen, perhaps even more strikingly. In one of the best pre- served and recorded, in Bedfordshire, dating from about the time of the Roman Conquest, the vault was a spacious 15 by 12 foot room paved with tiles, and against one wall were six large amphoræ of Roman fabric which, on the evidence of pitch still remaining in one, had contained *vino picato*. (The total capacity, incidentally, is equivalent to about fourteen dozen bottles.) The more solid delights of the feast were represented by two double-ended iron fire-dogs, and two roasting-spits, and an iron tripod and chains to hang cauldrons over the fire. There were fine Roman dishes and bronze cups, and the mellow close of the banquet is implicit in the bone flute that lay on the pavement. In this, and in the other similar burials known, we regain a vivid picture of the actual furnishings of a Celtic feast in the immediately pre-Roman Iron Age in England. The fire-dogs, with tall finials worked into stylized ox-heads in brilliant smiths'-craft, are particularly interesting, as artistically they seem likely to belong to the Iron Age B tradition, and may well indicate the presence of such west English smiths among the craftsmen encouraged at the Belgic courts.

The Catuvellauni seem also to have adopted another, and very important, piece of technical knowledge from the Iron Age B people, and that was the use of the war-chariot. There is no doubt, as one sees in reading the *Commentaries*, that Cæsar was surprised, and indeed somewhat alarmed, to find his forces opposing an army in Britain which fought according to what must have been to his legionaries a totally unknown form of tactics. Chariot warfare had been extinct in Gaul since the second century B.C.; nowhere in his campaigns had Cæsar encountered it, and his knowledge of his adversaries, the Catuvellauni, as a tribe but recently settled in Britain from Gaul would lead him to expect contemporary Gaulish tactics and weapons. He had sent over spies before his invasion, but they do not seem to have informed him of this unexpected technique of war. We have seen that archæology shows that the tactics of chariot warfare, brought to Britain by the Marnian chieftains in the third century B.C., survived in these islands (among certain tribes only, according to Tacitus) long after they had become obsolete on the Continent, and the Catuvellauni, themselves from the Marne region, may have preserved some dim tradition of kinship with those who had crossed to Britain two centuries before. However that may be, the military genius of Cassivellaunus or of his war-leaders must have been quick to appreciate the possibilities of this rapid, mobile arm, to adopt it, and either to draft into the Belgic army contingents of Iron Age B charioteers or to train a large and efficient fighting force in these traditions of warfare. In the generation between their arrival in the Thames estuary and their magnificent rearguard action in retreat from the Roman legions in 54 B.C., the Catuvellaunian war-chiefs must have made a far-reaching decision, and completely remodelled their army in accordance with the older British way of fighting.

The consolidation of power within the territory ruled by Cunobelin seems to have resulted in a *pax belgica* which prevented, or ruthlessly stamped out, intertribal dissensions, and a similar confederation was probably established in the north under the Brigantes. The grimmer side of the picture of autocratic rule is brought out in the iron gang-chains for slaves from Belgic sites— from the classical sources we know that slaves were among the exports of Britain at this time, together with corn and metals, fat-stock and hunting-dogs, traded against such imported luxuries as wine and probably oil, as well as pottery and bronzes. Much coasting trade must have been carried in the curraghs, sea-going boats with a skin of stretched hides, that Cæsar saw in southern England and which survive in western Ireland to-day.

Any discussion of Celtic Britain on the eve of the Roman Conquest, at the end of its prehistory and on the threshold of a time when history can give us some at least of the story, must include mention of those figures dear to romantic antiquarians since the eighteenth century, the Druids. Of these priests of the Celts much nonsense has been and still continues to be written: archæologically they are almost intangible, while the references to them in the classical texts are exiguous and sometimes contradictory. But the fact of Celtic religion, and of the hierarchy which administered it in Gaul and presumably in Britain, is an inescapable one which we have already encountered in the purely archæological field, for the preservation of chariots or the appurtenances of a regal banquet in a tomb are the direct result of certain religious views concerning the life beyond the grave.

It may be dangerous to generalize from the Gaulish evidence (which is more complete) when considering the Druids and their cult in Britain. But certain facts do seem fairly likely to be applicable to the whole range of Celtic religion, which in general seems to be a member of a related group found in regions where Indo-European languages were spoken in early times. Common to these religions is a priesthood—Brahmans, Flamens, or Druids — one of whose duties, in an illiterate community, is to memorize the corpus of religious teaching and to keep this oral tradition pure. Such was Druidic practice in Cæsar's time, and Sanskrit literature was handed down in this manner until the eighteenth century A.D.: with this went the similar achievements of the bards, whose repertoire included the pedigrees of the prince and his court. That Cunobelin was the son of Tasciovanus is archæologically evident from the inscriptions on the coins of the two rulers (though nowhere recorded in the extant classical texts), but there had been sufficiently good continuity among the Celtic bards for this relationship to be preserved in the pedigrees of the early medieval Welsh princes who proudly traced their ancestry back to expatriated Belgic princes who had fled north-west at the coming of Rome.

The Druids regarded their religion as already ancient in Cæsar's day, and apparently with some reason. There seems to have been much continuity in Britain at least from the Early Bronze Age, and in Berkshire an Iron Age homestead or village in the mixed A and B tradition had a circular earthwork shrine in the ancient manner; while at Stonehenge some structure, probably in wood, was contemplated or constructed on the eve of the Roman Conquest around the already ruinous stone temple on the site. The strong element of barbarity in Celtic religion must not be forgotten, for human sacrifice is emphatically attributed to the Druids by more than one classical writer, and the Roman extirpation of Druidism, so unlike the general tolerant absorption of a native cult into the accommodating Roman pantheon, was, as in Carthage, dictated by the necessity of stamping out such savage practices within the Empire. The holocausts of victims in wicker figures constitute a ceremonial cremation which is curious, and it might not be fantastic to recall the multiple cremations at Stonehenge and other Early Bronze Age shrines. And even the golden sickle which allegedly cut the mistletoe may have at least a Late Bronze Age origin, when functional sickles of bright bronze were in use.

The most famous appearance of the Druids in Britain is in the pages of Tacitus, where he describes their cursing the Roman army on the shores of the Menai Strait in Anglesey. In this island there were, on his authority, Druidic sanctuaries, and with the growing force of the Roman conquest of southern England many of the priesthood may have sought a refuge in North Wales. Recently, tangible archæological evidence of what can hardly be other than a votive deposit in some such sanctuary has come to light, in the peat-bed of Llyn Cerrig, a tiny lake near the western coast of Anglesey, where an incredible hoard of miscellaneous metalwork had been formed, and lay with the animal bones of sacrificial feasts. We know that the Gauls after battle piled up dedicated heaps of the spoils of war in consecrated spots: sometimes these were in sacred pools, and such deposits have in fact been found in Denmark where Celtic influence is perceptible. The Anglesey hoard included iron swords and their scabbards, spears and shield mountings; the metal fittings of war-chariots, and of the harness of the horses; gang-chains for captives, currency-bars of Iron Age B type, the mountings of ritual staves, and part of a bronze trumpet. Much of the metal-work was decorated in the finest traditions of the north-eastern and the south-western Iron Age B provinces, and it could be shown that every significant object in the hoard was of Lowland English origin, coming from an arc of country stretching from Yorkshire to Somerset, except for two objects (one the trumpet) from Ireland. The dates of the objects all lie between about 150 B.C. and A.D. 50, and all must have been deposited in this remote sanctuary before the arrival of the Romans in the island, constituting a remarkable testimony to the connexions by trade with the Iron Age B and C provinces of the Lowland Zone that the sacred communities in North Wales must have possessed. Rather similar votive deposits have been found at Carlingwark Loch, Eckford and Cockburnspath in the Scottish Lowlands, dating from the first or second centuries A.D., but containing some earlier objects.

.   .   .   .

In completing the outline sketch, so often blurred and incoherent, that we have been able to present in this short book of the substance of British prehistory, it only remains to indicate briefly the survival of prehistoric traditions on the fringes of Romanization in the first century A.D. The full force of the Roman invasion of A.D. 43 turned against the Belgic tribes of the south-east, now, after the death of Cunobelin, without an effective leader. 'Heretofore', wrote Tacitus (in Savile's translation), 'they were governed by kings, now they are drawn by pettie Princes into partialities and factions ... seldome it chanceth that two or three states meete and concurre to repulse the common danger.' Cunobelin had banished one of his sons; two others, Togodumnus and Caractacus, led armies against the Romans in A.D. 43. Both were defeated, but Caractacus escaped westwards and united the Silures and adjacent tribes into an anti-Roman front, and in this context the building or refortification of the hill-forts on the Welsh Marches, in what appears to be an eventual Iron Age A tradition, is significant. Some defensive line based on these forts seems to have been kept until A.D. 51, when Caractacus fought his last battle against the now insistent Roman power, to escape again and seek refuge with the Brigantes, whose pro-Roman queen, Cartimandua, betrayed him and handed him in chains to Ostorius in the following year.

The decisive Roman move north of the Humber was made in A.D. 71, when Cartimandua's policy had at last succeeded after the civil war with her husband, who led the local anti-Roman armies. In another decade Lowland Scotland was reached, and it seems likely on the archæological evidence that there was a migration of the descendants of the Marnian settlers in southern Scotland northward into territory until that time held by folk whose ancestors had built the *murus gallicus* forts, and who were probably within the Iron Age A cultural group. At all events, characteristic metal-work based on the Marnian traditions but to be dated in the first or second century A.D. now occurs within the regions north of the Firth of Forth and as far as Moray. In Scotland, and in other areas of the Highland Zone, Romanization can have affected the agricultural population of the countryside comparatively little—oddments of Roman pottery or glass were acquired by crofters or villagers, but the Iron Age traditions died hard, and it is when the pressure of Romanization is relaxed by the break-up in the Dark Ages that we see again the Celtic metal-smiths handling their material with the same consummate skill as they had before the Conquest, and with traditional styles that had not even then forgotten their Marnian and Belgic heritage.

BIBLIOGRAPHY

THE best general secondary source is V. G. Childe, *Prehistoric Communities of the British Isles* (1939); see also C. and J. Hawkes, *Prehistoric Britain* (Pelican, 1943); J. G. D. Clark, *Prehistoric England* (1940). For the geographical approach, see C. Fox, *Personality of Britain* (1944); for Scotland, V. G. Childe, *Prehistory of Scotland* (1935); Wales, W. F. Grimes, *Guide to the Collection Illustrating Prehistoric Wales* (Nat. Mus. Wales, 1939); Ireland, S. P. O'Riordain, 'Prehistory in Ireland, 1937–46', *Proc. Prehist. Soc.*, XII (1946). Good regional archæologies are H. Hencken, *Archæology of Cornwall* (1932); E. C. Curwen, *Archæology of Sussex* (1938); W. J. Varley, *Prehistoric Cheshire* (1940). For prehistoric agriculture, E. C. Curwen, 'Early Development of Agriculture in Britain', *Proc. Prehist. Soc.*, IV (1938); W. F. Payne, *Arch. Journ.*, CIV (1948) (forthcoming).

CHAPTER I—For archæological technique, J. G. D. Clark, *Archæology and Society* (1939); R. J. C. Atkinson, *Field Archæology* (1946).

CHAPTER II—For Lower Palæolithic, F. Zeuner, *Dating the Past* (1946); Upper, D. Garrod, *Upper Palæolithic Age in Britain* (1926); Mesolithic, J. G. D. Clark, *Mesolithic Age in Britain* (1932); ibid., *Mesolithic Settlement of Northern Europe* (1936). For fossil men and subsequent prehistoric types, C. Coon, *Races of Europe* (New York, 1939).

CHAPTER III—General statement in S. Piggott, *Neolithic Cultures of British Isles* (forthcoming); E. C. Curwen, 'Neolithic Camps', *Antiquity*, IV (1930); J. G. D. Clark and S. Piggott, 'Age of the British Flint Mines', *Antiquity*, VII (1933); V. G. Childe and S. Piggott, 'Neolithic Pottery of the British Isles', *Arch. Journ.*,

199

LXXXVIII (1932); V. G. Childe, *Skara Brae* (1931); S. Piggott, J. G. D. Clark, and others, 'Archæology of Submerged Land Surface of Essex Coast', *Proc. Prehist. Soc.*, II (1936).

CHAPTER IV—There is no detailed, up-to-date statement on the British Bronze Age; for Early Bronze Age sanctuaries, J. G. D. Clark, 'The Timber Monument of Arminghall', *Proc. Prehist. Soc.*, II (1936); R. J. C. Atkinson and C. M. Piggott, *Excavations at Dorchester, Oxon.* (Ashmolean Museum, forthcoming); for Beakers, J. G. D. Clark, 'Dual Nature of the Beaker Invasion', *Antiquity*, V (1931); Wessex culture, S. Piggott, 'The Early Bronze Age in Wessex', *Proc. Prehist. Soc.*, IV (1938); Late Bronze Age, C. Hawkes, 'The Deverel Urn and the Picardy Pin', *Proc. Prehist. Soc.*, VIII (1942); ibid., 'Three Late Bronze Age Barrows', *Antiq. Journ.*, XIII (1933); ibid., 'The Pottery from . . . Plumpton Plain', *Proc. Prehist. Soc.*, I (1935); E. E. Evans, 'The Sword-Bearers', *Antiquity*, IV (1930); other material in regional surveys.

CHAPTER V—There is again no up-to-date detailed statement, but for general classification, C. Hawkes, 'Hill Forts', *Antiquity*, V (1931); for Marnian invasions, ibid., 'The Caburn Pottery and its Implications', *Sussex Arch. Collections*, LXXX (1946); for farmsteads, G. Bersu, 'The Excavations at Little Woodbury', *Proc. Prehist. Soc.*, VI (1940); Glastonbury, A. Bulleid and H. St. G. Gray, *The Glastonbury Lake-Village* (1911–17); Veneti and hill-forts, R. E. M. Wheeler, *Maiden Castle* (1943); metal-work (Iron Age B, etc.), C. Fox, *A Find of the Early Iron Age at Llyn Cerrig Bach* (1947); Celtic art, E. T. Leeds, *Celtic Ornament* (1933); the Belgic settlements, C. Hawkes and G. Dunning, 'The Belgæ of Gaul and Britain', *Arch. Journ.*, LXXXVII (1931); C. Hawkes and M. R. Hull, *Colchester* (1947); Belgic coins and dynasties, D. Allen, 'The Belgic Dynasties of Britain and their Coins', *Archæologia*, XC (1944); for Celtic religion, T. D. Kendrick, *The Druids* (1927).

MUSEUMS

THE raw material of British prehistory is mainly visible to the public in museums or as the field monuments such as those mentioned in the book from time to time. The BRITISH MUSEUM (London) at present (1948) exhibits a selection of the more striking and important objects from prehistoric Britain; the NATIONAL MUSEUMS of WALES (Cardiff), SCOTLAND (Edinburgh), and IRELAND (Dublin) have large and representative collections from their respective areas. The University Museums at OXFORD (ASHMOLEAN) and CAMBRIDGE (ARCHÆOLOGY AND ETHNOLOGY) have important local material from the Upper Thames Valley and East Anglia; the CITY MUSEUM, BELFAST, represents Ulster, and the MANX MUSEUM, DOUGLAS, the Isle of Man. The PITT-RIVERS MUSEUM, FARNHAM (Dorset), has the outstanding results of Pitt-Rivers's work on Neolithic, Bronze Age, and later sites in the region displayed with scale models of the excavations. Noteworthy local museums are those at TAUNTON (the Iron Age marsh-village finds and much else); DORCHESTER (Bronze Age material from Dorset, finds from Maiden Castle); SALISBURY and DEVIZES (Neolithic, Bronze, and Iron Age finds from Wilts.); AVEBURY (Neolithic finds from Windmill Hill, Early Bronze Age from the stone circles); LEWES (Neolithic and Iron Age material from Sussex); COLCHESTER (finds from Belgic sites); NORWICH (Norfolk prehistory); SHEFFIELD (Bronze Age finds from Derbyshire moors); HULL (Neolithic and Bronze Age finds from the Yorkshire Wolds); YORK (Yorkshire prehistory including some material from Iron Age chariot-burials); and NEWCASTLE-ON-TYNE (BLACKGATE MUSEUM) (Northumberland prehistory).

INDEX

Printed in Great Britain by The Riverside Press, Edinburgh

GN805   .P5

Piggott, Stuart

British prehistory.

DATE	ISSUED TO
	19140
FEB -3	
FEB 27	

19140

GN
805
P5

Piggott, Stuart
British prehistory